SEX, LIES & P.I.'S

Ali Wirsche and Marnie Milot

Durban House

Printed in the United States of America

For information address:
Durban House Publishing Company, Inc.
7502 Greenville Avenue, Suite 500, Dallas, Texas 75231

Library of Congress Cataloging-in-Publication Data
Wirsche, Ali, 1955 -
Milot, Marnie, 1949 -

Sex, Lies & P.I.'s / Ali Wirsche and Marnie Milot

Library of Congress Control Number: 2007921882

p. cm.

ISBN: 1-930754-94-9

Second Edition

10 9 8 7 6 5 4 3 2 1

Visit our Web site at
http://www.durbanhouse.com

This book is dedicated to all the people who think they can cheat and get away with it.

Two-timing lovers beware...
We may be on your tail!

CONTENTS

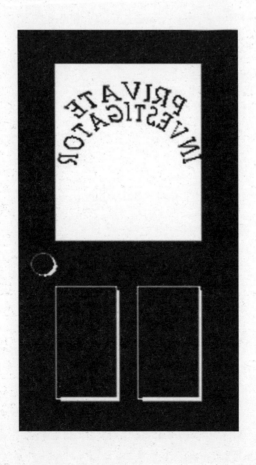

INTRODUCTION

"Are you those two ladies?" When our friendship began in 1973, we had no idea how powerful those words would be. Both of us married in 1974 and went our separate ways. Marnie and her husband moved overseas and started a family. Ali and her husband stayed in Calgary to raise their family. During Marnie's time in Greece, she had the opportunity to meet and work with a private investigator. The seed was planted.

In 1988, Marnie and Ali were reunited when Marnie and her family moved back to Calgary. Our first taste of investigating came later in 1989, when one of our mutual friends had marital problems. She had suspected her husband was having an affair and needed support. We fell head first into the world of deception and lies. We spent many nights following her husband and eventually confirmed the affair. From that point on, another friend recognized our talents and soon started spreading the word. Most women our age had much tamer hobbies. Our hobby had turned out to be "undercover surveillance."

Finally in 1995, while keeping our day jobs, we opened a home-based private investigation business called Backtrack Investigations Inc. To buy equipment we both skimped on groceries for our families and finally purchased our first video camera. Two women, happy and settled in their lives, turned their knack for sleuthing into a thriving, successful private investigation firm specializing in catching cheaters.

During the days, we managed full-time jobs, raised our families, and worked our business on lunch hours, nights and weekends. On our home computers we created letterhead, brochures, and business cards, while marketing ourselves. Every free hour was spent researching the private investigation industry at the local library. After enrolling in private investigation courses, we never looked back. The time came when we knew in our hearts that we had to quit our day jobs despite our own fears of losing that regular paycheck. We located reasonable office space. Our monthly rent consisted of cleaning the office and bathrooms, and buying and making the coffee. For this we had access to a loft office, computer, photocopier and fax machine. We found our office furniture in junk stores, lying in a back room, covered with dust. Many cans of spray paint revitalized the junkyard furniture. Most of our first consultations were conducted in donut shops, because our office was still unsuitable to bring clients into.

Shortly thereafter we were on a long-term surveillance in a residential neighborhood. While parked in front of a house, we had to explain to the homeowner why we were there every day. He was a carpet supplier and installer, and we struck a deal, while parked in his driveway, to carpet our office. We were on our way!

This book evolved from our experiences of owning and operating Backtrack Investigations Inc. Every story documented in this book has been from our actual case experiences. Infidelity cases account for 60% of our business. We have chosen infidelity (this real human aspect of life) to write about, because few enterprises fail as often and as traumatically as relationships. Most of what we have learned about the love triangle has been from our clients. Their stories (with their identities changed) have inspired us to document their truly emotional highs and lows, and our sometimes humorous encounters when dealing with infidelity.

THE AFFAIR IS IN FULL SWING

Living a double life. The classic lipstick stain, the earring or cufflink found in the car, or the new perfume or aftershave scent, and the old standby, "I've got to work late at the office tonight." Adulterers continually face the dilemma of becoming full-blown habitual liars. Explaining a certain item found in his or her car, perhaps, or absences at all different times, can become very confusing. We all remember as kids how our parents could catch us in a lie, because when you lie, you still have to remember what you said. Adulterers cannot remember everything they've said or done. It is virtually impossible.

A night out with our best friends brought up some bad memories of an affair my husband had had two years before and the possibility of it happening again. My husband talked about a recent movie we had seen. He told our friends how we both had really enjoyed it. I was shocked. I had never seen this movie! I excused myself and ran to the bathroom. When I regained my composure, I went back to the table and remembered very little about the remainder of the evening. The next morning, I phoned a private investigator, and within a week my husband was caught with his lover of two years ago. The affair was in full swing again.

Jean, married 7 ½ years

Adulterers' lies become mangled. One lie always leads to another. Even if they have been caught in a lie, they will try to change their stories to get out of another embarrassing situation. Adulterers are usually not in love, but in love with the fantasy. Having an affair can be an addictive, compulsive behavior.

The *Globe and Mail* newspaper reports that a Stanford University survey revealed that 20-40% of married women and 50-60% of married men have had at least one promiscuous liaison.

> *The naked chef? My husband cooks, but doesn't clean. After I returned from a weekend visiting my mother, the house was in its usual disarray. We'd been having problems, but in my ignorance, I never suspected an affair. As I was closing the garbage, I noticed two wrappers for T-bone steak. I asked him if he had had anyone over for dinner. Of course, he said "no one."*
>
> *I said, "Someone sure has been eating a lot of steak." He told me he got hungry at midnight and decided to have another steak. I waited until the next day and tried again. He changed his story and said he had the other steak the next morning for breakfast. He had forgotten his previous story. His affair was exposed.*
>
> *Marge, married 14 years*

Our most memorable case is the "Church Affair." A frantic call came in one day from a female, asking if we could do something a little out of the ordinary to expose the affair she was sure her husband was having. The day she hired us, she was in such a state that she had a minor car accident on the way to our consultation, and then almost ran over the investigator who was meeting her. For over a year, her husband had always been one to two hours late coming home from choir practice. He was the choir director at their church. It seemed he always needed extra practice with the pianist, even on weekends. She was amazed every Sunday how the choir could sound so awful after all that practice. Other members of the church had told her to beware of the pianist.

There was a crying room next to the vestibule in the church they attended. The crying room had a one-way mirror for the mothers to see the service, but the congregation could not see into the room. Our client was a secretary in the church, so she had access to the crying room key. With the church officials' knowledge, she sequestered us into this room an hour before choir practice began. There were two keys to this room: the key we had, and the other one, which our client had bent and left hanging in the church office so no one else could use it to gain access to the crying room.

The choir practice began at 6:00 p.m. and ended exactly at 9:00 p.m. They practiced one particular song over and over. We practiced that song along with them, and when they were done we knew the song as well as they did. Even to this day we can sing it word for word.

In the room were two wooden chairs, a creaky wooden bench and a small closet. While the choir was practicing, we could move around freely, but when the choir was gone, we found that the room was NOT SOUNDPROOF!

At 9:00 p.m. everyone left but our client's husband and the pianist. They put their coats on the front pew and walked out of the sanctuary to the basement, where we heard a door closing.

After about 45 minutes they came back into the sanctuary and stood in front of the crying room, embracing passionately. They actually leaned up against the glass and continued necking. After a half-hour of this, they put their coats on and left.

Our client had told us that when a certain light in the hall was off, it would be clear to leave. We waited for the light to go off and then crept down that long, dark hall. As we passed the staircase that led to the basement, to our amazement we heard voices in the basement. We couldn't believe they were still in the church! What should we do? Go back to the room? We knew we couldn't go back, so we flew out the back door, letting it slam behind us.

Later as we caught our breath, we couldn't quit laughing. We wondered if anyone had seen two middle-aged women running at full speed for three blocks. We called our client the next day and gave her the bad news. Her husband and his lover never heard the door slam. Since then our client and her husband have left that church, and they're working on repairing their marriage.

> *My husband was away on a business trip. I needed to speak with him and telephoned his hotel. When the front desk answered, I asked to be put through to "Mr. Jones' " room. The desk clerk said he wasn't in his room, but "Mrs. Jones" was just walking through the lobby, and would I like to speak to her? I said absolutely!! As soon as she said hello, I knew my husband's secretary's voice. I was broken-hearted and shocked. I never believed my husband would sneak behind my back and cavort with his secretary.*
>
> *Rita, married 21 years*

Stories always conflict in the midst of an affair in full swing. Adulterers can't keep their minds clear or focused when they are tumbling down that self-destructive path. They are constantly in a frenzied fantasy world. "Tom" told us his wife called him and said that she would be over shortly. He thought about what she had said and asked her, "Are you going to be over shortly, or are you coming home?" She had obviously forgotten whom she was   talking to.

> *My husband and I loved to go to Las Vegas. We were out for dinner with our best friends one night, and my husband made a comment about being in Las Vegas four times in the past two years. I spoke up immediately and said, "We have only been there three times." He argued briefly and then became silent, realizing that one of those trips was not with me. He then changed his story and said, "Yes, you are right. We have only been to Las Vegas three times." I knew I had him. After some in-depth research, I found that his secretary had made that extra trip to Las Vegas.*
>
> *Kelly, married 23 years*

Even careful adulterers can't cover all their tracks. It is usually a paper trail, unexplained absences, or a critical comment that catches them in their tracks. A change in sexual activity or no sex at all can be a signal that something is wrong. Our job is to prove or disprove our clients' suspicions. If you find receipts to a restaurant that you have never been to and your spouse denies ever being there, something is amiss. Sometimes adulterers can be very convincing in their lies. Admitting to having an affair is virtually impossible. If the adulterer really loves his or her partner, he or she sometimes even tries to create opportunities to admit the affair. We continually tell our clients that unless you have all your evidence and it is clear, adulterers will continue to lie. People cheat because they think they can get away with it.

> *My husband was the coach of our son's hockey team. A friend of ours was the assistant coach. They spent a lot of time at the arena and often sent the kids home with other parents so they could go over their coaching strategies. Eventually I became suspicious and hired an investigator. We found out they were doing their own kind of coaching.*
>
> *Lorraine, married 14 years*

Jenny needed our advice on her situation. She had recently begun to suspect her husband of an extramarital affair. He was a racquetball enthusiast and played two to three times a week. The day before she called us, she had snuck into her husband's car to snoop while he slept. Finding nothing, she decided to wash his gym clothes that were kept in his gym bag in the trunk of his car. She couldn't remember ever washing them. She retrieved his gym bag, and with ice picks poking at her heart she realized they were squeaky clean. Someone was either washing them, or he never played racquetball! On the scheduled night of his racquetball game, we followed him from his house. After driving down many back alleys, he finally pulled up at a house and a woman discreetly snuck into the passenger seat. They went to a coffee shop and held hands in the corner while gazing into each other's eyes. Racquetball was obviously not his game of choice.

My wife was again at her computer. She was so immersed in what she was doing, she didn't hear me come up behind her. I glanced at the screen and saw a love letter. The words leapt out at me. "I miss your touch. See you soon, Darling." She realized I was behind her, looked at me and started to cry. She said that she was sorry, the relationship had started out casually, but had escalated. Before any more damage was done, we sat down and started talking like never before. Now we are both looking forward to the future, together.

Jack, married 4 years

"I need proof!" cried Jim. For the second weekend in a month, Jim's wife was working overtime. In the mail that day, addressed to Mr. & Mrs., was a thank-you card from a hotel about five miles from their home. The clues were impossible to ignore, so we were on the case. We followed her on a night that she had told Jim she had a late business meeting. She left her office at 5:00 p.m., leaving her car in her parking spot, and walked six blocks to a hotel. In the lobby was a gentleman waiting for her. They went into the lounge hand-in-hand. After a few drinks, they made their way upstairs to a room. We followed them to get the room number. We then called the hotel from the lobby, asking for that particular room number, but pretending we had forgotten the person's name and would be terribly embarrassed. The desk clerk sympathized and told us the man's name. As it turned out, the man worked for the same company as Jim's wife and frequently traveled to our city on business.

No matter how well adulterers think they are covering their tracks, everyone having an affair eventually makes a mistake. Guaranteed.

Remorse is another sign of an affair. Guilt comes in many forms. Joan's living room was filled with three hundred roses from her husband. Three hundred roses? What could possess him? It had to be guilt. His fateful mistake in his affair's being revealed was his overwhelming feeling of guilt. This flower child was busted when we followed him to his lover's house.

I knew my marriage was in trouble. Mark had been spending a lot of time at the office. He always worked late, and never came home on time. He insisted I was crazy when I asked him if he was having an affair. He looked at me like I had slapped him and asked how I could think such a thing. Soon after, my husband and I were invited to a cocktail party. A woman approached us and introduced herself. My husband seemed very tense all of a sudden. He asked if he could get us both a drink. He came back with white wine for me and a gin fizz for her. The mistake he made was, he never asked her what she drank; he knew. After the party, I confronted him and he tried to talk his way out of it. I reminded him of his slip with knowing what she drank. He just sat in the car and stared straight ahead, and finally admitted a long-time affair.

Lorna, married 21 years

TELEPHONE TAG

The telephone is instrumental in the life of an affair. It connects the two lovers and disconnects the partner left alone. WHICH CALLS ARE YOU RECEIVING? Are they the irritable ones, like "I'm working, I'll be late, don't wait up for me"? If the adulterer cannot be with his or her lover, they will definitely communicate by telephone, and often!

Jill had innocently installed a caller-display on her telephone the day before but had not discussed it with her husband. Jill had never given much thought to her husband's always working late.

That night, her husband called and said how sorry he was, but he had to work late again. However, her caller-display showed Relax Inn, not his office. Outraged, Jill hired us to find out what kind of work was going on at the Relax Inn. The next week we waited in the parking lot for him to drive in. We walked in right behind him and headed straight to the elevator. He pushed the 4th floor. So did we. We all got off on that floor, and so as not to appear that we were pursuing him, one of us stopped to tie our shoelaces. We then walked slowly, so we could see what room he went into. Jill wanted the confrontation at the hotel and was anxiously waiting for our call. Our job was over when Jill arrived with a bottle of champagne and knocked on the hotel room door. We never heard if anyone actually drank the champagne or wore it.

TIPS ON LANDING THE LINE—If your mate phones the lover from the office, there is no way to track these calls. At home, the clues are easier to follow. If you leave the room and your partner picks up the phone, walk back in unexpectedly. If you leave to go on an errand, return to the house quickly, as though you forgot something. Chances are the connection has been made on the phone. If the phone is quickly hung up, something is amiss.

1. **"ME TOO"**—Have you ever entered a room and your mate quickly ends the conversation with "ME TOO?" What is YOUR mate's response when you say "I LOVE YOU?"

> *I often heard my husband in the middle of the night, talking in the living room. I would get up and he would be on the phone. I would go back to our room, and when he came back to bed, I would say, "Were you on the phone?" He said it was the T.V. and not him that I had heard.*

This went on night after night. After one of his late-night calls, I pretended to be asleep. When he came to bed, I waited until he was snoring. I crept down to the living room and pressed redial. A very sleepy voice answered, saying, "Darling, I need my sleep. I'll see you tomorrow night." With the yellow pages on my lap, I sat up all night waiting for business hours so I could call an investigator. I had him followed after work that day. He phoned me from the office saying he would be working late and not to wait up for him. He led the investigators directly to his love nest. The story unfolded that he had a mistress and had settled her in an apartment that he paid for. He finally admitted a five-year-long relationship. He moved out and into his love nest. She can have him. I only wait for the day when he phones her and says not to wait up.

Marilyn, married 28 years

2. **HANG-UP CALLS?**—Does it only happen to you? If your mate just left, the lover is calling to see if your partner is on his or her way. There may be a change in plans. Perhaps a date was broken and the lover is checking to see if your mate is at home with you.

3. **PAGER**—When your mate's pager rings in your presence and he or she does not return the call, ask yourself why. Check for coded messages, e.g. "222" may mean, meet me at 2:00 p.m. at the usual place.

My spouse's pager would go off very late at night and he would ignore it, saying it was not for him. One night while he was sleeping, I checked the page. The next day, I phoned the number and said I had a delivery for her from (I gave my husband's name). Of course, I was not present when she thanked him for the flowers. He did admit his affair to me.

Patti, married 6 years

4. **CELLULAR PHONE BILLS**—They tell the whole story. The bill has a list of all the numbers, times, and dates called. Where do the bills go, home or office? If they're going to the office, WHY? If you have access to the cell bills, check each one carefully, especially the numbers called directly before or after your number. Normally if an affair is ongoing, your partner will phone you first. This is to reassure you that he or she is still busy at work. The next step is to immediately phone the lover to arrange a meeting. Another test is to phone your partner's cellular immediately after leaving the house. Chances are it will be busy.

My wife would constantly be going out to the garage. One day I followed her, and she was on her cellular phone in her car, talking. I did not let her see me. I checked the bills when they came in, pinpointing that particular day and time. I found an unfamiliar number not just once, but many times. I confronted her, and she tearfully admitted a long-standing affair. She left me and took our two children. He left his wife and three children. Their affair only lasted six months after that. Now five children are left without an intact family.

Walter, married 10 years

5. **E-MAIL/INTERNET**—Check the computer if you have access to your mate's password. This is an easy way to communicate, but an even easier way to destroy the evidence.

I noticed my wife was spending an unusual amount of time on the computer in the evenings. She eventually confessed that she had been chatting on the Internet for several months and had fallen in love with a stranger. How could I compete with a machine? She kept up the exchange for a period of time, much to my dismay. Then one day when I came home, I noticed the computer had been moved into the basement and put in a box, where it is going to stay.

George, married 6 years

6. **HOTEL PHONE BILLS**—If your mate travels, the hotel bills are a valuable piece of information. Hotels list all local and long-distance numbers called from a room. Hotel bills are very easy to obtain. Wait a few days after your mate arrives home and then call the hotel. Pretend you are doing the expense account and you have lost the original hotel bill. Have the hotel fax or mail the bill to a neutral location. The phone bill will be virtually the same as the cellular phone bills, displaying all the calls made. Take into account the numbers directly before and after

your own. You will receive the first call: "I'm beat, I'm going to bed, and the meetings were boring. I had a very long day. Kiss the kids and the dog. I'll talk to you when I get home." The next call will be to the lover. It will definitely be more than one minute. It may go something like this: "I miss you, I wish you were here. I can't stop thinking about you. I need your arms around me. Next time I want you to come with me. Love you lots, can hardly wait to see you."

My husband has his cell phone attached to his head. He is constantly on the phone. One night he was coming home very late and called me to ask if I needed anything from 7-Eleven before he came home. When he arrived home about ten minutes later, he put his cell phone on the table and went to the washroom. A power came over me, and I grabbed his phone and pressed redial. Our home phone number should have been the last number called, but it wasn't. I made a note of the number. He went to bed and I again pressed redial, but he had cleared the number already. I dug through his cellular bills with the detailed billing, noting the number called and the time and day of every call made in that month. The number I was looking for came up right after he would phone home, time and time again. Further investigating with the help of professionals gave me the truth I needed. The affair had been going on for years.

Connie, married 15 years

The telephone is one of the major elements in an affair. It takes planning, rearranging of schedules, and phone calls for that clandestine meeting. A new way to cheat is text-messaging. Text-message your lover and tell him or her to meet you at 5:00 pm. There are no out-going calls, and text messages aren't retrievable.

LOVERS AND OTHERS

Society is facing a moral dilemma. What is acceptable in sexuality? Are our attitudes changing toward gays? For the majority of people, that is not a world that they are living in.

Now, what if that world has somehow crept into your world? COULD YOUR PARTNER BE GAY? DO YOU REALLY KNOW THE PERSON YOU ARE MARRIED TO OR LIVING WITH? HAVE YOU IGNORED YOUR MATE'S POSSIBLE ALTERNATIVE LIFESTYLE?

COMMON SIGNS OF A GAY LIFESTYLE

1. Leaves at night with no explanation.
2. Socializes or works with other gays. ("Gaydar")
3. Reads body-building magazines.
4. Appears homophobic in certain settings.
5. Dresses meticulously, color-coordinated. Spends a lot of time in front of the mirror.
6. Performs sex very mechanically or not at all.
7. Displays a sensitive personality.
8. Job category.
9. Type of music and Hollywood stars (Liza Minelli, Cher, George Clooney, Brad Pitt, Mathew McConaghey)
10. Can't quit looking at people of the same sex.
11. Loves to shop and decorate.
12. Artsy and bookish.
13. Works out at the gym.
14. Very white teeth and very tanned body.
15. Top of the line furniture and the house is immaculate.
16. Looking at Internet gay websites.
17. If still married, he or she can appear very edgy.
18. May use an alias when in clubs.
19. Frequents steam rooms.
20. It's all about the look.

How can I ever forget our last holiday together? Married 10 years with two small children. Now my loving and adorable husband is openly living with another man. Our sex life hadn't been the greatest for the past year, but this holiday was going to change everything. My husband had booked the entire trip to celebrate our wedding anniversary. When we checked into the hotel, I did notice a lot of gay men, but I was naive. Even when I found out there was a gay convention at the resort, I still did not catch on. One night my husband woke at midnight and said he couldn't sleep and was going down to the bar for a drink. I got up at 1:30 a.m. and realized he wasn't back. I went down to the bar, and what I saw will stay with me forever. My husband was kissing and holding hands with another man in the bar. My mind raced back to the events of the week and of our whole marriage. Since then he has confessed that for five years, he has been in gay relationships.

Sonya, married 10 years

Every case is different and doesn't turn out as we would imagine. During an investigation, we habitually assume the affair is with a member of the opposite sex. However, we have learned that in this profession, you never assume anything.

One night while we were on a case, following a man for his suspecting wife, we got a very big surprise. Our suspecting client's husband was a body-builder type who worked out daily in a gym. The night of the investigation he immediately left his home, drove to a donut shop and went into the washroom. We waited and waited. All of a sudden, we noticed a well-dressed woman getting into the driver's seat of his truck. We immediately realized he and the well-dressed woman were the same person. He was a cross-dresser. His wife had hired us because she had found some articles of women's clothing in his vehicle. He wasn't having an affair. He was the other woman!

Of the cross-dressers we interviewed, we found that half of

them were heterosexual and the other half dressed like a woman to pick up a man. Often transvestism does not become overt until marriage. Usually the wife doesn't know of the cross-dressing until well into the marriage, when the husband expresses an interest in female clothes. Frequently, the way the wife discovers something is amiss is when her husband is in the basement trying on her clothes. Cross-dressing continues throughout life with various degrees of frequency. Cross-dressers are often very scrupulous and exact in their habits.

My marriage ended after 23 years, when I discovered my husband was a transvestite. I could not believe the evidence put before me. I hired a private investigator to uncover the truth. My husband was a tall, well-built man who worked construction. He was the last person in the world I would have suspected to dress up as a woman. What a shock when a brochure came in the mail addressed to my husband. It featured large size ladies' shoes with 5"-6" heels. I also found a membership card to a gay club that had been updated only two days prior. I decided I needed hard evidence, because I knew I would have a hard time believing my husband had another life. I had him followed, and within a week I was presented with pictures of my husband sporting a blonde wig, beautifully tailored blue suit and high heels. Once I could leave my bathroom, and not have to listen to my heart pound, I presented my husband, whom I love dearly, with the pictures. He sat back, stared into space and finally told me that he thought that if his 23-year marriage was every-thing it should be, and everything he wanted it to be, he wouldn't want men.

Kim, married 23 years

George knew something was going on with his wife, but hav-ing to travel on business, he was not home enough to put his finger on the problem. We followed George's wife for two solid weeks. She didn't seem to be doing anything out of the ordinary. She would get together with a female friend and go to lunch, to the gym and shopping. They always had our client's two young daughters along.

We were starting to think that nothing was out of the ordinary until two weeks into our investigation. On a Friday night, we again set up a surveillance and followed George's wife and her female friend to a bar. On the smoked glass door the sign said "Gays and Lesbians only." Nervously, we slowly opened the door and walked in. It was our first encounter in such a place, and our eyes were opened. On the dance floor, dancing provocatively with her female friend, was George's wife. George left the marriage, but his two young daughters are living with their mother and her friend.

I had been married for six years to a wonderful man. One day I had the flu and stayed home from work. I turned on the television to watch one of those day-time talk shows on television. The topic was: IS YOUR WIFE OR HUS-BAND GAY? They had a list of ten things to watch for. My world fell apart in those few minutes it took for me to read the list of signs. My husband fit every category. I called my sister and told her my fears. Her response was very remarkable. She said that she had always thought my husband could be gay, but it had been none of her business. I had written down the list from the program, and when my husband came home, I showed it to him. He was embarrassed, but truly relieved. He hadn't wanted to hurt me, so he had stayed in the marriage. We split amicably. My husband died of AIDS three years later.

Justine, married 6 years

How is it possible to know someone so well and yet have never understood something as basic as his or her sexuality? Married homosexual persons may find themselves in chains of love and association that are hard to dismiss. They have difficulty imagining how deeply their conflicts are hurting their partners. Many people have mixed feelings of guilt over leaving their partner or never having been all the partner needed.

If you suspect that your partner is gay, you may not necessarily find him or her hanging out in gay clubs. His or her straight domestic and social lives often leave little time for a gay social life. When gays or lesbians are unable to resist their homosexual urges, they are more likely to pick up gays in bath houses, or private gay social clubs, where they can exercise their duplicity.

In the course of our many investigations into the gay community, we learned that most gay people discover their sexual nature in many ways and at different ages. Some may be happily married for years when they find abruptly that their sexual relations with their partners leave them unsatisfied. The realization may come as a shock. An overwhelming feeling of loneliness is an invariable part of that shock.

Disclosure day does come: there will be heavy fallout, such as sadness, pain and a sense of loss.

IS YOUR LOVER MARRIED?

 A distinct tan line where a wedding band once was. Do you know the signs of a married lover? What would you do if you found out your lover is married?

 Lovers who contribute time and emotion equally to a relationship have a better chance for happiness and a long-lasting relationship. What if your lover is married? How much will he or she be able to contribute? One thing you are likely to never have is the opportunity to be together on an important holiday. Whom do you think your lover will be with on Thanksgiving Day, Christmas, New Year's or Valentine's Day, that special day for lovers? You will be seen on the unimportant days or whenever your lover can fit you in. If you like spending holidays alone, you will enjoy many of them with a married lover.

A married lover already has one commitment: the spouse. What if your married lover also has children? Are you competing with swimming lessons, soccer practice, dance lessons, and school functions? Guess who makes the sacrifice? An affair with someone who is married will consist of unfulfilled promises. Usually married adulterers are more interested in quantity, not quality.

I was a mistress for nine years. I actually had talked myself into believing I wanted this affair that was totally noncommittal. Our relationship was comfortable, even though I spent many weekends and holidays alone. Holidays are not easy for adulterers. One day, to my horror, when he called me to tell me he couldn't come over that night, I realized his excuse was similar to when he used to call his wife from my place. I had a dilemma. I was the mistress and had no holds on this man, but now he could be cheating on me! Marriage is more convenient than a love affair. Being a mistress is inconvenient. I never gave any thought to what I was doing to his wife and children. I hired an investigator to find out if he was cheating on me. He was seeing some fluffy blonde from his office. The day I broke off the relationship, I found out I was pregnant with his child. He wanted no commitments. He reminded

me of our deal made many years before. I
totally screwed up, but I have an adorable
baby boy. My son does not have a dad to
grow up with, but my son and I do have
someone to spend holidays with. Each other.
                              Trina, involved 9 years

How many times have you asked yourself, Could my lover be married? Married lovers are very passionate, romantic, gorgeous, yet mysterious. If you have not asked your lover any of these questions, maybe you should.

1. WHY DON'T WE EVER GO TO YOUR PLACE?

  a. My place is too small and my roommate is a slob.
  b. I am living with my parents until I get enough money
       together to get a place of my own.
  c. I live in the country. It's too far to drive.

2. WHY DON'T I SEE YOU MORE OFTEN?

  a. I'm putting in a lot of overtime at work.
  b. I'm happy with the way things are.
  c. I work out those nights and can't see you.
  d. I have to visit my mother Friday night.

3. WHY CAN'T I PHONE YOU AT HOME?

  a. My telephone has been disconnected. My roommate
       didn't pay the bill.
  b. I'm never there anyway.
  c. I'm really hard to get ahold of. I work crazy hours.
  d. You can always leave a message on my cell phone, or
       page me.

4. WHY HAVEN'T I MET ANY OF YOUR FRIENDS?

    a. I don't have a lot of free time for socializing.
    b. You're all I need.

5. WHY DO WE SELDOM GO OUT?

    a. I'd rather stay in and have you all to myself.
    b. We have everything we need right here.

6. HOW COME I FOUND A COLORING BOOK IN YOUR CAR?

    a. I lent my car to a friend, who has three kids.
    b. It's mine. They were handing them out at a restaurant I
        was at.

Your lover has finally confessed that he or she is married. Now what? Think back to the beginning of your relationship. How many lies did you hear? What is the commitment history? If your lover often talks badly about the opposite sex, or confesses to two broken marriages, then the commitment history is not great. It may not be long before you are no longer in the picture.

Laurel became suspicious because of the infrequency of our dates and my vague answers to her questions. She kept pressuring me into spending more time with her. I was torn. I wanted Laurel, but I couldn't give up my family. It all ended six months after it began. My wife and I had planned a trip to the zoo with the kids. Laurel happened to be there with her sister and niece. She looked at me

with tears in her eyes, but just kept walk-
ing. My heart stopped for fear of being
found out. My wife never suspected. I felt
so guilty. I hurt Laurel, but I also could
have hurt my wife and kids and torn
apart a perfectly great family.

Joe, married 11 years

If you have accepted the terms of a married lover, then you have to learn to live with it while the affair lasts. A married person who cheats might say, "I'm telling my wife in six months that I am leaving her." Or "As soon as my youngest is out of school, I'm leaving and we will be together. Be patient, it's not that easy. We will be together soon, I promise." If you are content to make these sacrifices for your married lover, then keep your expectations low, and you will have fewer disappointments.

I had been dating Brian for six glorious
months. I couldn't believe that a doctor
was in love with me. I didn't see him
often, but when his electric blue eyes
looked at me, it took my breath away.
Brian and I met in a park near my home
and across from the hospital where he has
an office. Our casual meetings led to a
dinner date. Brian was a great comfort
and always knew the right things to say.
The only problem was, he knew every-
thing about me, and I was learning so
little about him. There was a certain
aloofness about him, and he had an elab-
orate excuse every time I questioned him
about his personal life. After a distressing
long weekend when I never heard a word

*from him, I confided in a friend about my
mysterious doctor. She suggested I hire an
investigator to locate his home address. To
my amazement, Brian had a home in the
suburbs, and to my further disbelief, a
wife and two children. When I confronted
him with my evidence, he was shocked
and furious that I had had him investigated behind his back. I felt like such a
fool for falling into his trap, but at least I
only wasted a few months. It could have
turned into years.*

Cynthia, involved 6 months

Gloria feels that she wasted her childbearing years on a married man. Her lover was extremely wealthy and extremely married.
The affair endured for ten years. During the last six months of the
affair she had noticed subtle changes in their relationship. Their
morning rendezvous became more infrequent. Whenever she
called him at work, he was always busy. Her main connection with
him was through his cellular phone. Recently, however, it was
always turned off. Whenever she confronted him, he always had an
elaborate excuse.

One dark, dismal morning we set the surveillance up. Parking
our surveillance vehicle behind his house, we saw his headlights
turn on. Weaving in and out of traffic, we finally arrived at a hotel.
He squeezed his Cadillac Escalade into a spot and sauntered into
the side entrance. In the lobby he met a gorgeous redhead about
ten years younger than Gloria. She had been replaced by a younger
woman. At 40 she was alone, but what she really wanted was marriage and children. It is hard to believe, but some people enjoy the
intrigue of a married lover.

This is the affair in reverse. The married woman who wouldn't leave her husband. Many times I tried to break off the relationship with my lover, but I just couldn't. When I finally told him that I was staying with my husband, he broke if off. I firmly believe that we still love each other and always will, but it is over now. This was not just an affair of the heart, but an intellectual stimulation and common bond that I have never experienced before. It is really sad and hard to take that my two-year affair is over. I loved being married and I loved the excitement of an extra-marital affair. He realized that the affair wasn't fulfilling enough for him and he wanted to move on. I don't blame him. He has to go on with his life without me.

Melanie, involved 2 years

If you are having an affair with a married person, the best advice we can offer is, don't change anything in your life. Don't make any rash decisions that will affect you financially. Emotionally you have already been affected. Buying property together or changing careers to have more time with your lover could prove disastrous.

Having an affair with a married person affects more lives than just your own.

ASTONISHING ADVICE FROM A
SEASONED ADULTERER

1. Only use cash.
2. Keep the sex alive at home.
3. Never have an affair with someone who has less to lose than you do.
4. Always vacuum your car after your liaison. (Those long blonde hairs!)
5. Use the same shampoo or soap you use at home.
6. Carry two cell phones. (One for the spouse, one for the lover.)
7. Never take sample bottles or matches from the hotel room.
8. Leave your vehicle at the office and take a cab or walk to your rendezvous.
9. Only book day rooms at hotels.
10. Push two floors when you enter the elevator of the hotel to thwart any possible spies.
11. Always get a room at the end of a hotel corridor. (Less eyes to see you.)
12. Both parties need to have similar expectations and goals for the relationship.
13. Don't let the affair consume your life.
14. Only see your lover during the day. (What could you possibly be doing if you are home every day at 5:00 pm?)
15. If you do have to use a credit card to take your lover out, use two different cards; split the amounts evenly so it looks like only one person ate.

DANGEROUS DESIRE

Whether it is a co-worker you are fascinated with, the guy at the gym with the perfect body, or the person on the airplane next to you that you can't take your eyes off of, everyone gets the urge to bite the forbidden fruit. How many times have you heard someone say, "I wonder what she would be like in bed?" or "I'd give anything just to spend one night with the guy across the hall." Fantasizing can take you into a wonderful dream world, but carrying out your fantasies can take you into an unbelievably bad nightmare. Daydreaming about someone other than your mate will slowly start to disintegrate your relationship. An affair can be a real possibility.

According to statistics, it is no longer the seven-year itch. Recent surveys have shown four out of ten couples who approached five years of marriage had filed for divorce by the time their five-year anniversary approached.

Has your relationship been on rocky ground lately? Maybe

you have felt a certain deadness in your marriage. You have not had time or possibly not taken the time to work on your commitment. A critical aspect of "Dangerous Desire" is when two people have slowly drifted apart and are feeling forlorn. This is when they both are unguarded, and a seemingly innocent relationship can turn into adultery.

Perhaps you both enjoy golf, but you haven't golfed together all summer. Your sex life has been basically nonexistent. While driving to work you conjure up all sorts of plans to make things right. As soon as you get to work, you plan to phone home and suggest dinner and a movie. You arrive and your boss asks you to stay late. You arrive home late and your partner talks about someone special he or she works with. This name has come up in conversation a lot lately. Apparently the friendship happened because the other person was so easy to talk to. NO HARM DONE???

Even if there hasn't been any intimacy yet, three is a crowd. Thoughts often turn into actions. We all share a bond with our mates, and knowing that their most intimate and private thoughts and feelings are being conveyed to others makes us feel uncomfortable. Is your partner hearing from someone else what he or she has been longing to hear from you? Sharing emotional thoughts only strengthens the bond of desire.

> *My wife and I are career-oriented. We wanted to save money and then start a family. As our careers took hold, we kept putting off the family. I had a very demanding job, and I let it run my life. My wife was promoted very rapidly in her company and started to travel frequently. We weren't together enough to start a family anyway. After one of her trips, I found a card lying near her suitcase. It read, "TO A SPECIAL FRIEND."*

With my hands trembling, I dared to open it up. I'll never forget the pain in my heart after reading the words inside the card. "Thank you for taking the time to listen. We've been good for each other in the midst of our loneliness. I know it was the right thing to do last night, stopping before we went any further." I'm a 35-year-old male who never cries. Would you believe I cried for hours and hours? I confronted my wife later. We talked about a lot of things that were missing in our frenzied lifestyle and promised to make amends. I know that card saved our marriage.

Jason, married 6 years

Innocent flirtations can be a mask for loneliness. You can be lonely whether single or married. One of the first questions we always ask a client who suspects an affair is happening: Is your partner a flirt? It's very difficult to be in a relationship with someone who is flirtatious. We consider flirts to be the most susceptible to having affairs. A gorgeous woman coming on to your husband in a bar can spell trouble.

Most people don't get up in the morning and plan to have an affair that day. Something has to be prompted for it to happen. Emotionally, maybe you haven't been there. If a person's needs for intimacy haven't been met, resistance is low, and sometimes sparks of desire can turn into flames of passion. Don't think it can never happen to you, because it can happen to anyone.

All relationships need nurturing to grow. We all remember that feeling of falling in love. Those feelings will not last forever. You have to continually look for common interests and take time for each other. Setting aside time for more intimate conversations can build a better relationship. A romantic dinner, a walk in the park, or a special card can do wonders.

> *My husband was in the habit of compar-*
> *ing me to his secretary. She was 11 years*
> *younger. I realized I had gained some*
> *weight since the birth of our four chil-*
> *dren. Whenever I thought of buying*
> *something, the kids needed something.*
> *The day he suggested I have a tummy*
> *tuck and try slicking my hair back was*
> *the day I phoned him at work and told*
> *him there was an emergency at home. The*
> *emergency was our marriage. I talked*
> *about his criticism of me, and he talked*
> *about how my appearance had changed.*
> *Certainly my self-esteem was low. We are*
> *now communicating, and he no longer*
> *talks about his co-worker. We decided to*
> *join a gym together, so now we get a*
> *babysitter and thoroughly enjoy our time*
> *together. My husband was in the state of*
> *"Dangerous Desire."*
>
> *Hillary, married 18 years*

Seemingly harmless actions often have negative consequences. These actions truly have lives of their own and eventually build more secrecy, remoteness and distance between partners. If you keep pushing your mate away with fantasies, your emotions are not fully with your partner.

There is a fine line to cross from friends to lovers. Sometimes relationships develop over a long period of time. It is important in the beginning stages to set boundaries. If you never question your partner's whereabouts, attitudes and actions, your mate might feel you've given permission to do just about anything. Don't give your partner a chance to get involved in a relationship that started as "just friends." Many platonic relationships have turned into unexpected affairs. Feelings can change or grow deeper if your partner is spending a lot of time with a "friend." If that person's name continually comes up in conversations, it already may be more than a friendship.

I knew my husband was infatuated with our neighbor, who is gorgeous. Every weekend someone on our block was having a party. I consider my neighbors who live across the street some of our best friends. I stayed home to raise our four children, at my husband's insistence, and really would not have wanted it any other way. My gorgeous neighbor has three children and is an executive with a large firm. She mentioned casually at one party that she wanted to start jogging in the mornings, but had no one to join her. My husband took the bait. They started jogging three times a week to start. Then it was just about every morning, and then they started going after supper. I finally was so frustrated that I sat my husband down and had a heart-to-heart with him. He honestly did not know how I was feeling. I told him my concerns, and after a few weeks of continuous talking, he found a different jogging partner, an overweight male friend of his. I don't know if anything had happened, but I was concerned that they certainly had the oppor-

*tunity to take their relationship to the
next level.*
Toni, married 18 years

In all relationships, people need to set boundaries as to what is acceptable behavior for them. If your partner is uncomfortable with your going out with your co-workers for drinks, then it is something you need to discuss. Inappropriate actions can sometimes lead to inappropriate results. If you start fantasizing about someone other than your mate, you have to decide immediately whether you want to put all your energy into thinking about this other person, or into figuring out what is wrong with your relationship and then working to restore it.

LUNCHTIME LIAISONS

One out of five people has an affair with someone he or she works with. Is it happening to you? Where does your partner spend most of the day? WORK! Three or four nights alone in the office can create an atmosphere for an affair. You can do things to prevent your partner's having a romance at work. If the affair is already happening, there are many ways you can find out very quickly, if you have done your homework.

Get to know your partner's co-workers. If you are invited to a company picnic or Christmas party, ATTEND! If your husband is an engineer and he is explaining to you some design he has created, obviously you will not understand it completely. However, it is important for you to show interest by listening. If your girlfriend has just completed a major sales presentation to a difficult client, give her your support. Have dinner ready when she walks exhausted and haggard in the door. If your mate is not getting support at home, he or she will look elsewhere! LISTEN TO YOUR PARTNER!

I had absolutely no interest in my girlfriend's work. She worked as a reporter for a local television station. I am a high school teacher and had my own problems to deal with. She had expressed to me often that she was unhappy with her job because she felt her boss didn't treat her with respect. She was ready to take on some bigger and better stories and knew she could handle them. She talked about her unhappiness constantly. I always told her she was smart and I knew that she could work it out, and eventually those big jobs would come her way. Obviously a male co-worker must have been more sympathetic and sensed she needed someone to talk to. He approached her and asked if there was anything he could do to help. She told me that they started going for a drink after work just to talk. After several weeks of talking over drinks, they ended up at his apartment. I eventually hired an investigator because she had completely shut me out, and I knew we had major problems. I can't put all the blame on her; she tried to talk to me, but her new lover was there when she needed someone, and I wasn't.

Kent, together 3 ½ years

It is easier for people in certain professions to begin and to continue an affair. If your partner travels out of town frequently, especially to the same place, an affair can go on for a long time without your knowledge. The first question we ask a new client about conducting a possible surveillance on his or her mate is, "What does he/she do for a living? Is it a nine-to-five job, or does he/she freely come and go at will?"

A traveling mate can provide opportunities for the person left at home too. If your job takes you out of town frequently, phone home at odd times to check up. If your partner works in an office, drop in unexpectedly on occasion. Let everyone in the office know who you are! Get to know someone in your partner's office. You don't have to be a lifelong friend, but you may need that person sometime.

We were trying to keep tabs on Fran's husband during a case. He was busy and involved in meeting after meeting and lunches all day long. It was very hard to keep track of him. Fran finally befriended her husband's secretary, and with the secretary's help guiding us to where he was hour-by hour, day after day, we caught him at one of his "meetings."

If your partner talks about someone more often than you care to hear about, you'd better start listening. Try to arrange a few lunch dates with your partner; see how often you are refused. Phone your partner Friday at 3:00 p.m. and ask him or her to meet for a drink. If you are unsuccessful, his or her Friday afternoon may be booked with someone else.

My husband was a very successful businessman. He left his regular job of 20 years and started a new company in the telecommunication business. He asked a female associate from his previous company to work for him. He knew she was intelligent and she could benefit his com-

pany. He talked about her great business mind all the time. Suddenly, I never heard a word about her anymore. My husband decided to expand into another country, and the two of them were away together for two months. My 20-year marriage was secure, or so I thought. When my husband arrived back home, I sensed something was different about him. About six months later, his female associate that he had brought into the company moved to the new location of the business to look after that franchise. I was actually relieved to see her go.

My husband still had to travel and spend time at the business, but I never suspected anything. During one of those business trips, I thought I would surprise my husband at his hotel and enjoy the weekend away with him. He always stayed at a particular hotel, and I booked a flight and headed down. I was very excited and looked forward to my little adventure. I walked into the hotel, and since it was mid-afternoon, I knew my husband wouldn't be there. I explained to the desk clerk that I was joining my husband, and she gave me a room key. My heart still stops when I remember what I encountered when I entered the room. My husband and his associate intertwined on the bed, with clothes strewn from one end of the room to the other. I don't even remember coming home, but somehow I made it. My husband did not.

Shelly, married 20 years

Persuade your partner to take time away from work. Plan a vacation together every year. If you have kids, get a babysitter and plan a quick weekend getaway without them. If he or she is stressed out from work, you be the one to do the consoling. Encourage your partner to take part in family activities outside of work. If he or she golfs every week with people from work, and goes to the bar with people from work, that doesn't leave a lot of time for you. There is a life outside the office.

If your mate is in a social office and a lot of time is spent in the company of co-workers, personally and professionally, an affair can often happen. One of our client's possessive husband's reasons for his affair was, "The bills and mortgage were overwhelming. I felt by having an affair, it took the burden of the world off myself. I felt like somebody else, with no problems." The affair was with a co-worker and a friend of our client. Our client was not able to deal with the affair and filed for divorce. He now has more bills to add to his portfolio.

During the Christmas office party season, the bells are ringing in our office. The telephone calls we receive are all very similar. "My husband is going to his company Christmas party, and I am not invited! He tells me spouses are not invited this year." A lot of parties are in public places, and we also attend as uninvited observers. At one Christmas function we were hired to watch Tim's wife, but it was a private gathering. Listening to the people gathered waiting to go in, we realized that nobody actually knew everybody. The party consisted of three branch offices from different cities, and everyone was celebrating Christmas together. All we did was stand in line with the rest of the group and write a name on a name badge, and no one was the wiser. We had a perfect vantage point to watch the action unfold, and it did.

When Trudy hired us, her main concern was how her husband acted in a social scene, not to mention that she had found a long red hair in her bed. His office was having a party in the back of a large restaurant, and the gathering was visible from our table. We had a picture of Trudy's husband and immediately identified him. He was at a table with five other people.

To someone else's untrained eyes, there was nothing out of the ordinary. What we noticed, however, was the body language between her husband and a red-haired woman seated next to him. Their chairs were pulled closer together than the others at the table. She would always lean into him while talking and casually brush his arm. During the evening, the office manager was giving out awards, and everyone stood in a group to listen to the announcements. He positioned himself at the back of the group, and it did not take long before the same woman from his table made her way back there. His arm went around her shoulders and when she won her award, he gave her a hug. They stayed in that same closeness for 15 minutes.

Trudy wanted a phone call when he was leaving the office party. We told her what we had seen, and she confronted him when he walked in. He of course denied it and told her that the incompetent investigators she had hired were watching the wrong guy. He tried brainwashing her into believing him, and she even questioned us to make sure we had the right guy. Of course, we had a video to substantiate our report. Only when he saw the video of himself and his office honey did he admit to anything.

> *My wife's company's barbecue last summer was held in a cabin 20 miles outside the city limits. A long hike was planned for everyone. I was a very avid hiker and passed most of the group early on. My wife and her boss managed to return 45 minutes later than everyone else. I felt a pang of jealousy, but of course I dismissed the incident as nothing. For the next month, she worked late at least two nights a week. When I finally asked her*

about it, she said a lot was going on at work; they had a big project due. Soon, I noticed very subtle changes in my wife. She started dressing like she was going out at night. I noticed her wearing very tight fitting-clothes. She kept coming home later and later, and finally, after repeated attempts to talk to her to no avail, I hired an investigator. Her boss had an apartment in the downtown area, and that is where the investigator followed them to. Her boss had been call-forwarding the office number to his apartment. I asked for a divorce. About eight months after they were found out, my wife was out job hunting.

Steve, married 7 years

If you fall into an office romance, you'd better start dog paddling, because you are in for rough waters. Once the desire wanes, in a week, a month, or possibly a year, you will have to face the prospect of daily interaction and the consequences of your actions. Marriage is a reality and is always at the mercy of intrusions. The reality of fidelity is the ability to remain loyal in spite of contradicting values. Affairs are a fantasy. Having an affair postpones dealing with real life.

Large and small companies are becoming more concerned about co-workers making more than copies in the photocopy room. The conversation around the coffee cart is not the company's bottom line, but the boss's interest in his secretary's bottom! Some employees are putting in unauthorized overtime in the elevator, the boardroom, and the boss's leather couch. Employers have become very vigilant about office romances. Sexual harassment lawsuits can sink a small company. Typically it can cost between $100,000 to $200,000 to defend, according to experts. A spurned lover will stop at nothing if he or she feels they were passed over for a promotion or treated unfairly by a former lover and supervisor. Relationships are hard enough to maintain without all the exposure an office romance dictates.

Janet thought she had everything in life she wanted. She had a great job and had just put a down payment on her first house. She knew her supervisor was interested in her. He invited her for a drink, and she took the bait. Their hot romance took them to the stock room—making love on a stack of paper—to a wild encounter behind a tree at the company picnic. Six months later, Janet was huddled in the bathroom crying. She had seen her lover pay more attention to a co-worker. How could that person have been promoted when she was next in line? Confiding in another co-worker revealed she was his second office affair. Feeling betrayed and humiliated, she spoke to his boss and confessed the affair. Not able to endure the gossipmongers, she quit her job in humiliation. A tragic ending to a promising career.

The next time your co-worker brushes you in the hall or your eyes meet across the room, return your eyes to your computer, take a deep breath and invite your spouse for lunch. Some office couples become so de-sensitized as to how they're being judged, they lose all perspective at work.

If you are dumb enough to start an office romance, you'd better establish clear get-away routes from the very beginning. Planning an end to your torrid affair is about as romantic as planning your own funeral. Job and career repercussions often follow an office break-up.

My husband and I worked together in a large firm. I caught my husband having an affair with a co-worker. He knew this was against company policy, but he wasn't getting any air to his brain! I was able to intercept messages between the two of them. Knowing the boss would be interested, I re-directed their love messages to the boss's phone.

Kirsten, married 4 years

10 Rules For Office Romance

1. Date for genuine reasons. Because you like each other—not for power.

2. Evaluate pros and cons.

3. Know what you want from the affair.

4. Have a clear exit route.

5. Be discreet!

6. Don't date a married co-worker.

7. Don't make decisions based on emotions.

8. Read the company guidelines.

9. Keep your lovemaking out of the boardroom.

10. Don't have a relationship with someone who has more to lose than you do.

THE DREADED MID-LIFE CRISIS

Regaining lost youth: the little red sports car, a ponytail with whatever hair is left—or a new hair color—younger clothing, jogging, a new membership at the gym, eating salads. These are a few of the classic warning signs of a possible mid-life affair on the horizon.

At 45 years old, my husband started acting strangely. For the last ten years he had been gradually losing his hair. I had told him over and over that it did not bother me, but he actually became obsessed with the hair loss. One day he came home with a hairpiece that included a ponytail. I thought it looked ridiculous, but he was absolutely thrilled with his new look. He then did something that was so off-the-wall, I still shake my head. He sold our family car and bought a two-seater sports car! In my rage, I asked him how in the world our family could possibly go anywhere together in that? He didn't have an answer. Our lives were never the same again. Eventually, he moved out and now is dating a much younger woman, only a few years older than our eldest daughter. Our kids are horrified, and I am a single mom.

Elaine, married 25 years

Anyone can have a mid-life crisis of some kind, but not everyone has to have a mid-life affair. It is common knowledge that as people age, we don't feel as attractive as when we were younger. A man may not have all the hair he possessed when he was twenty years old. Women tend to worry more about weight gain and body shape.

In our profession, we have met many men and women in their 40s trying out the dating scene again, just to test the waters. Keeping yourself fit and looking good may not prevent your spouse from having an affair in mid-life, but it can be an excuse for you to have an affair yourself. How many times have you heard this: "If my wife or husband would have taken better care of her/himself, I wouldn't have had to look elsewhere." A dreaded catch phrase is "I NEED TIME OUT." Whenever our clients tell us their spouses need "time out," inevitably we find full-blown affairs.

My husband recently celebrated his 50th birthday. It wasn't a great celebration.

Over the last several months, he had become very dissatisfied with his life. He wasn't sure if he even wanted a wife and family anymore. He asked me for a "time out." I didn't really even know what that meant. He assured me that there was no other woman, just that he needed to be by himself for a while. I felt this was such a selfish act on his part, because we had four teenagers to raise. After months of virtually not talking to any of us, I told him to take his "time out," because I couldn't stand the atmosphere in the home. He found a small furnished apartment and moved in. We had a hard enough time paying all our household bills, much less the rent for a furnished apartment. I never really knew if he had another woman, but I suspected as much. After four months of this nonsense, I confronted him, but he still felt he needed his time alone. His "time out" is now permanent.

Janet, married 26 years

When we are young and in love, we don't know how we will be feeling about ourselves and our partners when we reach mid-life. We are all invincible at a young age. With age comes maturity. With maturity comes awareness and self-understanding. Mid-life is a critical period when people sometimes attempt to prove to themselves and others how youthful they have remained. This urge to boost their egos can sometimes lead to affairs. Often we leave one set of problems, only to discover a whole new set. As bad as relationships seem sometimes, the person who is struggling with this crisis needs a jolt to see that there was no one else he or she valued as much as the person whom he or she gave up. The right ingredients were always there. The grass isn't always greener on the other side. YOURS MIGHT JUST NEED MOWING!

WHAT'S WRONG, HONEY?

"What's wrong, honey? What did I do? What can I do to make things better? I'm sorry if I did or said something wrong. Why don't you talk to me anymore?"

Do any of these statements sound familiar? Have you been asking yourself these questions or making these statements, not knowing why you even have to verbalize them? These are very common indicators that all is not well in your relationship. When one partner begins to cheat on the other, certain patterns emerge. Often the cheating partner will project the guilt and deceit onto the other partner. She/he will withdraw affection and attention, and in some cases, commit acts that will deliberately sabotage the present relationship.

Let's deal with the most common effect—withdrawal. A partner who is cheating feels tremendous guilt. Because of the standards we set in all relationships, this is a common emotion. We expect truthfulness and faithfulness in our relationships. These are the bricks we use in building trust. As a house needs a sturdy foundation; so does a partnership. When one partner cheats, the truthfulness that was the foundation of the relationship has been damaged. Cheating weakens the basis of trust. Once the foundation has been weakened on any structure, the remainder of the structure is in danger of collapsing. Both partners soon recognize that there is severe structural damage and also know that this damage is sometimes irreparable.

How can partners who are cheating on their mates consider themselves to be honest? When you were dating, you told each other secrets you wouldn't even have thought to tell anyone else. This was because of the trust you had in each other. The cheating partner now must withdraw that trust because he/she has broken it.

My wife was acting strangely, and I kept asking her what was wrong. She would never answer my questions. I was totally frustrated. One night when I couldn't sleep, I made the decision to find out what was going on. I felt so guilty, but I went through her purse. I found something so totally unbelievable that my breath was knocked right out of me, and I don't even remember how long it took for me to regain my composure. Imagine my shock at finding a container of contraceptive foam, especially since I had had a vasectomy three years prior! I sat up all night, holding the container and conjuring up images of my wife. As the sun rose, I was still sitting in the kitchen, waiting for my wife to awaken. I heard her stirring, and I put the container on the kitchen table, awaiting her response. She looked at it, and then at me. She immediately tried to lie by telling me she had just bought it because she wanted to try it out sometime to see what it was like. I just looked at her like she was a total stranger, and then calmly walked out. The investigators I hired confirmed my suspicions. I filed for divorce.

Tom, married 10 years

A physical injury that hurts our exterior is similar in nature to the results of an emotional injury brought on by cheating. The trust that built the relationship has been shattered. A cheating partner begins to think differently about honesty. The cheater is the one who is destroying the agreement. When the adulterer goes out to meet the lover, he or she knows ahead of time what the plans are and exactly why the partner is left at home. Trouble begins to creep in, and when the guilty partner goes out for an innocent reason, the interrogations begin. The foundation is starting to crumble. When someone closes off emotions toward you, the normal response to the question, "What's wrong, honey?" is "Nothing is wrong, leave me alone." At that point you know that EVERYTHING IS WRONG!

I kept asking my husband, "What's wrong, honey?" when he started staying out later than usual and coming home in a very strange mood. In reply to my questions, he would say, "Nothing." His schedule eventually became more erratic.

When I would ask him where he had been, he always said, "Working." I continued to press him, saying, "What is wrong? Can I help? Please talk to me! Together we can work it out." He didn't seem that interested in working on our relationship. I even bought a book on mid-life crisis, thinking I could help him through this difficult time in his life. Little did I know he was getting his help elsewhere. The investigators I hired uncovered my husband's extracurricular activities. I found the evidence that confirmed the suspicions I had been denying. I presented it to my husband, who could no longer say "Nothing is wrong." In fact, everything he had told me was a lie. He moved in with his divorced girlfriend. I am very bitter toward him. Now when he asks me "What's wrong?" I say, "Nothing!"

Patty, married 21 years

Does your partner act detached from the relationship? Is there little desire to satisfy your needs, or possibly, does your mate avoid contact with you altogether? Are there other interests outside the relationship? Deterioration of love is a process marked by phases and turning points in a person's life. Events in our lives certainly change our behavior and attitudes. Our lives consist of a series of circumstances, some satisfying and some adverse. Not all of us deal with adversity the same way. Whether our experiences are gratifying or undesirable, we take what we learn and mold it into our lives. Adversity makes some people stronger, while others want to hide under a rock. You hear horrific stories about people going out to the corner store for milk and never returning.

There is always a reason for someone to be indifferent. It does not necessarily mean that your mate is having an affair, but unless you know the cause, the relationship can easily collapse.

Most of our clients, when they come to us, are distraught. They usually feel out of control. Often when a mate is cheating and is confronted, he or she usually responds that his or her partner is the crazy one and imagining everything.

During an investigation, if we have found nothing to validate an affair, our client will feel exonerated. He or she can then go home and instead of feeling helpless, take control of the situation and find the solution to their relationship quandary another way. Continually accusing your mate of an affair will sometimes lead him or her down that road. When we prove affairs during our investigation, our clients then know they were not imagining it and they're not really crazy.

My wife started having late business meetings. Her company had a lot of salespeople from out of town, and they would meet at a certain hotel for these meetings. She would always tell me whom she was with. As the months went by, she was having more and more late meetings. When she would come home, she would be very indifferent to me. I would try to talk to her and ask her what was wrong, but she would basically ignore my concerns. She always talked about one particular business associate. Eventually, I phoned the hotel where their meetings were always held, waiting until I knew the salespeople had checked out. Using the name of the gentleman my wife talked so highly of, I casually said that I

*had just been at their hotel, but had inad-
vertently thrown out my hotel receipt, and
without a copy, I would not be able to
recover my expenses. They faxed me a
copy. The room was registered to Mr. &
Mrs... with room service for two dinners
only, and of course, champagne. What a
shock! That was only the beginning. A
month later, I still had not confronted my
wife, but as it turned out, I didn't have to.
My wife sat me down and told me she
had good news and bad news. The good
news was that she was pregnant, and the
bad news was that the baby was not
mine. In hindsight, I realized my wife
had always told me whom she was meeting, in hopes that I would never suspect
her affair.*

Mark, married 9 years

Finding out why your partner is discontented is imperative to
saving your relationship. Maybe remoteness is not because of an
affair. Only when you have all the facts can you make an informed
decision on what route to take in saving your union. But asking the
question, "What's wrong, honey?" will likely never reveal the truth.

KNOW WHEN TO HOLD 'EM,
KNOW WHEN TO FOLD 'EM

Is there a more humiliating experience than discovering that someone you love and care for and have devoted your life to is having an affair? As one of our clients said, "I feel like my guts have been ripped out by a two-by-four." You ask yourself the same questions over and over: "Could I have prevented this? What do I do now?" Tears generally flow in the initial consultations with our clients, both male and female. Our experience has shown that our male clients fall the hardest. All we can offer our clients are our hearts, and some sort of peace, by giving them tried and true advice on what their next step should be. Recovering emotionally is very hard to do. Try to talk to someone you can trust. Whether it is a friend or a relative, you will need to confide in someone. It always helps if someone shares your pain. Sometimes a kind word or a comforting shoulder can do wonders.

Unless you have definite proof, you could blow it by confronting your mate too soon. An affair is almost always denied when you have not been able to substantiate your accusations. Adulterers can look you right in the eye and deny everything. Just because someone else saw them with someone or they weren't where they were supposed to be at a certain time, they will continue to lie if you don't have all your proof. If you do not want to end the relationship immediately, be ready for the consequences. Unless you have caught them in the act, adulterers will continue to distort your accusations and tell you that you are crazy.

Calming down and being in control will enable you to formulate and set forth a plan of action. Finding questionable receipts in a purse, wallet or briefcase can prove invaluable. If these receipts are from places that you have never been, then you have something. It is also important if you can photocopy these receipts and then put them back where you found them. Before you ask your mate any questions, the ploy is to know the answer. The most common answer to a questionable receipt is a business lunch or a dinner with a client. Sometimes adulterers will even say that the particular receipt is not even theirs.

My husband was a salesman and was always closing deals late into the night. He would come home at 3:00-4:00 a.m. I would often ask him where he had been. His response was that he and clients were having coffee and discussing a deal at a well-known pizza restaurant. He would be out three or four nights a week and always came home late. I bought his story for months, until one day a friend and I went to that same restaurant for lunch. On the door were the times of operation. It closed at 11:30 p.m. every day. I confronted my husband, and he said they had probably just started closing early. I phoned the restaurant, and they of course confirmed that they had always closed at that time.

Lynda, married 14 years

Jeannie was married to a lawyer. Before we revealed his affair, we knew that we had to have everything documented and videotaped. For sure he would find a loophole and deny the affair. We told our client, "Be calm, act as if nothing is going on. Don't change anything about your behavior." She did exactly as we said. We followed him for three successive days at lunch. The first day he went to lunch with his staff. The next day he met a female at a restaurant near his office. There wasn't really too much interchange or body language that we could detect from our vantage point.

The third day he picked up the same female in his car. They drove to a restaurant and stayed in the car kissing and embracing passionately for ten minutes before going in. We had all the action on video and gave our client the evidence. For nearly three months, she stayed in the marriage, being the best actress she could, and never said a word. During that time, before she finally confronted him with her evidence, she was putting her finances in order, slowly building her assets, and hiring the best divorce lawyer in the city.

I was taking our children out to my parents' cabin on the lake for the weekend. I phoned my wife from my cellular phone when I arrived. She said she was in a hurry and had to go. I didn't think too much about it. The next morning, I turned on my cell phone, and I had a voice mail message. I retrieved the message, and what I heard blew me away. It was not meant for me, obviously. It was a conversation my wife was having with a male, and it was taped on my voice mail. When I had called the previous evening, our call was never disconnected properly. She had a habit of not hanging up the phone all the way. What I heard was my wife and her lover talking about their plans for that evening. I could hardly stand to listen to the rest of the conversation. I phoned an investigator from my parents' home and had my wife followed the following evening. With the video of them together and the taped conversation, I had all the proof I needed.

Malcolm, married 11 years

The biggest mistake our clients make if they suspect an affair is following their mates themselves or having friends and family follow them. This can lead to ugly confrontations and still might not get all your proof. Hiring a professional investigator and getting evidence on video, whether it is holding hands in public, kissing in the park, or your partner's car parked in front of a motel, shows that physically and emotionally, he or she is with someone else. If you have a picture of your partner snuggled up in a lounge with someone, and you get the story of a hard day's work, what are you going to believe? Until you have all your undeniable evidence, DON'T PLAY YOUR CARDS!

SWEET REVENGE

Revenge does feel good! It is a powerful feeling to have the last word. If a relationship has been scarred by an affair, the scorned partner has to have a way of redeeming all the suffering he/she has endured and somehow restore the damaged identity. What is a more dynamic way for redemption than revenge?

Many people need that moment of adrenaline when their vindictive emotions boil over. We have all heard the sayings, "Hell hath no fury like a woman scorned. An eye for an eye, and a tooth for a tooth." It seems that mostly the female sex has this powerful need for revenge. Many of our clients have been scorned, and their partners are now looking behind them with their one remaining good eye!

An anonymous phone call led our client to a restaurant where her husband was wining and dining a woman. She asked three of her friends to join her in some "sweet revenge." The four of them sat in a location of the restaurant so as not to be seen. They ordered four bottles of the most expensive wine and ate lavishly. When the bill came, they asked the waiter to give it to the gentleman over in the corner. Looking very confused as he was presented with the bill, her husband looked up and saw them waving goodbye.

Julie came to us to end the deception her husband had been living. After meeting with us to receive our report and video, she went home to find her husband of 20 years in bed with the other woman, a co-worker. Her husband had never witnessed such fury from his wife, who now was a "scorned woman." She had changed from a quiet kitten into an enraged tigress. Julie had always doted on her husband, whom she felt had become lazy over the years, but she loved to spoil him. She confided in us that she had never set any boundaries with her husband, so he easily fell into an affair.

She set her plan in motion. After the scene she created at home, her husband and his lover left the house. She gathered all her husband's dirty laundry, put it in a garbage bag, and first thing the next morning, proceeded to her husband's office. When she walked in the office dragging this bag behind her, a few heads turned. The receptionist told her that her husband was in a meeting in the boardroom. Pushing past the stunned receptionist, she boldly walked into the boardroom. Julie went directly to her husband's lover and said, "Have it all, I've been doing his dirty laundry for 20 years. Now it is your turn." Julie walked out, drove home and packed the rest of his clothes and put them on the front porch. She told us she felt ten feet tall, basking in the power of vengeful rage.

> *A holiday in a Caribbean island was not the greatest place to find out that my life had taken a new twist. My husband and I and another couple had planned this hol-*

iday for years. On our second night there, my husband was apparently trying to phone his lover, unbeknownst to me. He obviously could not make the connection. The hotel desk kept trying for him, and while he was in the shower, the desk called and said the party my husband had been calling was now on the line. Once I heard the female voice on the phone, I felt like I had been hit in the head with a brick. The voice was unmistakably a good friend of mine, recently divorced. I hung up the phone and asked them to disregard my husband's request. The next day and for the remainder of the holiday, I charged freely on his credit cards. The day we left our island paradise, my husband was checking out of the hotel, and his credit card was declined. Our friends had to pick up the tab. I watched the scene unfold from my vantage point behind a palm tree, feeling truly vindicated.

Carol, married 7 ½ years

Forgive and forget? Not likely. Most of our clients want some kind of vindication after they have been rejected by their partners. When you get to know someone, you always know his or her weak points and what will wound the most. Adulterers always feel guilty and remorseful, and consistently want to forget their indiscretions ever happened and get on with their lives, with no consequences. Unfortunately, most humans aim at vindication by attempting to build themselves up. Others do it by tearing down their enemies. Anyone who has lived with betrayal typically wants widespread public humiliation for his or her partner. In most affairs, there are usually more people that know about the affair before you do. That, of course, makes the hurt even more powerful. You have probably been out socially with friends and acquaintances who knew your partner had been sleeping with the enemy.

> *The husband of the woman my husband was having an affair with called me. It was unbelievable. He had reason to believe that the two of them had gone away together for a week. My husband had told me that he was going fishing with a few of the guys. I did some sleuthing and found literature on a resort in Mexico, where he had apparently gone without his buddies. I then drove to the airport and searched for three hours until I located his car. The weather that week was extremely hot. Knowing how he liked fish, I bought some. I went back to the airport and opened his car with my set of keys and deposited the fish on the front seat of his beloved car. Rotten fish for a rotten liar.*
> *Lina, married 12 years*

Pete wanted revenge when he found out his wife was unfaithful. He told us something just came over him, and he had to get some sort of revenge. His wife was a cosmetician. One night when she was out, he took all her makeup and wrote on all the bathroom mirrors and hallway walls with a few unsavory comments. He then moved out to leave her with the mess she found herself in.

My husband was unfaithful to me one too many times. I thought I could change him, but how many times can you forgive? He was a high-powered businessman. He always bought the best suits and cars that money could buy, even if it meant borrowing. When I finally realized the situation my husband was in, I was truly mortified and enraged that I had let it happen again. I wanted to inflict some misery into his life. I opened up his closet and, with scissors in hand, I cut all the legs off his suits and deposited them in the front seat of his car. It felt wonderful.

Julia, married 32 years

When the investigators phoned and told me my husband was going away with his secretary for the weekend, I cancelled all of his credit cards, saying that they were stolen. I hope she had to pay for their cozy rendezvous. Since they flew to their getaway, my husband's car was in our garage. I never really was thrilled with the color. We had some old paint left over, and I dumped all of it over his car! I honestly felt a sense of power and absolutely no regret.

Josie, married 19 years

Fumbling with the keys and hearing the phone ring, we burst into the office and grabbed the phone on the last ring. On the line was a woman with a southern accent. Her husband had suddenly announced he was moving to our city and informed her he wanted a divorce. He told her he had outgrown her. No other explanation.

She wanted to know the real reason. He originally told her that he was living in a basement suite alone, and his buddy and wife lived upstairs. If she called, she could leave a message with his buddy's wife. During our investigation, we quickly ascertained there was no buddy and no basement suite. He had definitely set up a love nest.

*I caught my husband red-handed. One afternoon, a dear old friend phoned out of the blue, saying she was at a downtown hotel, and asked me to join her for lunch. I had never been to this particular hotel before. I walked in and located my friend. As we sat down, to my horror, I saw my husband with his arm around an acquaintance of ours, coming into the restaurant. Obviously, he knew her as more than just an acquaintance. He was so enthralled with her, he never even noticed me. I hardly tasted my lunch. I went home and asked our pastor for advice regarding my husband's indiscretion. His answer to me was that if my husband wanted to learn from his mistake and ask for forgiveness, he had the perfect way for him to redeem himself. Our pastor wanted my husband to stand in front of the congregation, including our four children, the following Sunday and disclose his shame. After many long heartfelt talks with my husband, we decided to save our family and marriage. He swallowed his pride, and that Sunday he took his place in front of our friends and family, and spoke from his heart.
Peggy, married 23 years*

Brent's wife drove to a sleazy motel. We watched her park her car in front of room 167. Before knocking on the door, she reapplied her lipstick. The door opened slightly, and she went inside. We called our client, who immediately wanted to catch her in the act. We don't recommend this, but he said he only wanted some harmless revenge. He pulled up and got out of his car. Using keys he had for his wife's car, he drove her car away, leaving his car in the parking spot where she had previously been parked. Three hours later Brent's wife sauntered out of room 167. She stopped dead in her tracks as she spied the car parked in her parking spot. She walked around the car and looked at the license plate. Surprise! Sweet revenge!

WASTED REVENGE

Ron was distraught over his wife's affair. It was so devastating to him that he decided the only way to deal with it was by having an affair himself. On his second night with his lover, he realized that he felt no happiness, just guilt. After breaking off his own affair, he hired us to follow his wife for six months. Ron became very obsessed with his wife's whereabouts and wanted to know every move she made. He arranged a lunch with her almost every day and smothered her with affection. It took a long time to rebuild the trust in their marriage. Two years have passed since the affairs, and Ron tells us that they are still working on the marriage; but their marriage is getting stronger.

911—CALL ME

Jacquie was not the revenge type, but she wanted to have some fun. She initiated several calls to her husband's lover's pager, leaving the telephone number of the city dump and various male escort agencies. Not stopping there and getting caught up in the thrill, she paged her dear hubby eight times during a business meeting, leaving the girlfriend's number. We hope the pager and the girlfriend were disposed of.

VIDEO HIGHLIGHTS

Claire's indelible words to her husband on their wedding day were, "Treat me with dignity and respect, and I'll be your friend and lover forever. Betray me, and I'll never let you forget it."

Claire's husband didn't remember those words when he was sleeping with her best friend. The proof was in the video that we had provided. Claire and her husband hosted a party for all of their friends. They recently had been on a fantastic voyage to the Far East and had told everyone that the trip had been captured on video. To Claire's best friend's and her husband's horror, the video was of the two of them coming out of a motel holding hands and kissing. To everyone's amazement, our client remained very calm. The two guilty parties were in shock. There was no denying this affair or justifying their behavior. An overwhelming feeling of empowerment came over Claire, and she knew she had enacted the perfect revenge.

TOP 30 UNBELIEVABLE LIES
TO DENY AN AFFAIR

1. It was the craziest thing. The condom wrapper you found in my car blew in the window.

2. It was the craziest thing. The condom wrapper you found in my car must have dropped out of the mechanic's pocket.

3. It wasn't me.

4. It only happened once.

5. It hasn't happened yet.

6. We are just friends.

7. I have the condoms in my glove compartment because I use them as finger gloves in case I come across an accident on the road.

8. I have contraceptive foam in my purse because I bought it by mistake.

9. Guess what, honey! Your vasectomy didn't work. We are having another baby.

10. The reason I have two bracelets in my suitcase is that I thought I might lose one, and then I would have a backup gift for you.

11. The reason there is a woman living at my house is because she is a squatter. I came back from vacation and there she was!

12. The reason I have a prescription for Viagra is that I heard it helps male pattern baldness.

13. I have a huge project at work, so I have to get my own apartment to concentrate.

14. I have lipstick in my briefcase because I found it on the sidewalk and picked it up so someone wouldn't trip over it.

15. I have no idea what you are talking about.

16. I was in jail.

17. I have a hotel key in my pocket because I found it on the sidewalk. I haven't had time to return it.

18. The blonde hair on the passenger seat must be from the mechanic who worked on my car.

19. I don't know why you couldn't get ahold of me. My cell phone must be dead.

20. I lost my cell phone.

21. I have a laundry basket full of clothes in my car because someone left it beside my car.

22. I have a gift bag in my back seat because I found it in the parking garage.

23. I found those boxer shorts with the happy faces on them kicking around the office and brought them home.

24. The reason I don't have any baggage tags on my suitcase is because before I leave the airport I always remove them.

25. I don't know why I have a receipt for diapers.

26. We were in the hotel room talking about you.

27. I was drunk.

28. The hair you found in the bed was my son's. He must have stayed here while you were gone.

29. Last week I was 50% ready to come back to you. Now I'm 80% ready.

30. You're crazy.

www.happilyeverafter.com

Cyber-sex is dangerous! Internet chat lines are a liar's paradise and perfect for a clandestine affair. Online lovers are becoming the most recent divorce trend and a tremendous part of our private investigation business. Chat lines often lead to a real affair. What people fail to realize is, if they do not trash the trash, that electronic love letter is still on the computer!

Where else can a person make false claims and instantly become taller, wealthier, and of course, single? Internet infidelity is a very real, destructive problem that is changing our ideals of trust, sex and intimacy. Virtual infidelity can blossom into the real thing and make adultery easy. It is hard to imagine that the power of a computer can break up a relationship. A committed person can now choose from a variety of philandering options with a few quick clicks. An online affair allows you to escape the everyday emotional static of that face-to-face relationship.

Having an affair online allows a person to know only a small part of his or her potential lover. During an Internet affair, a person meets a possible mate in the absence of intuition. When a person goes online and chats, he or she eventually start sharing intimacies and secrets and is far enough away and unconnected to daily life. Many people believe online affairs are harmless, because there is no touching. But a full-blown affair could be starting from your own home in your "electronic bedroom."

"Cyber-love" develops from a combination of fascination and loneliness, and it can become addictive. In cyber-land, a person can engage in wild fantasies. You can already see his beautiful blue eyes or her gorgeous smile. In cyber-space, there is no need to fear AIDS, pregnancy or lipstick on the collar. Computers are often instrumental in carrying out or seeking out extramarital affairs.

> *I had been married for 18 years when my husband Brad bought our first computer. As time went by he spent more and more time surfing the Net. He told me he was downloading games for our kids. Eventually he was on the computer until 4 am. One night, when he finally went to bed, I got up and turned on the computer. I found a series of love letters stored in his e-mail. The last one was a message from a woman who was looking forward to another meeting with my husband! My husband tried to make me understand that he had found the love of his life. I of course was devastated when he left me for his online lover.*
>
> *Carla (married 18 years)*

During an affair, people will sacrifice their reputations to satisfy their own needs. On the Internet, most people are not who or what they claim to be. People tend to be deceptive about their professional and marital status, their assets, and most commonly, their age. When you meet face-to-face, you can evaluate each other through nonverbal clues, such as gestures, clothing and expressions.

A troubled husband called our office, concerned about his wife of ten years. They had three small children, and his wife was up all night on her computer. What he found on it shocked him. There were many suggestively sexual letters from one particular man. From the content, it appeared their romance was love at first e-mail, but they had not met in person yet. We recommended our client keep his eyes open and call us the next time his wife was going out by herself. It didn't take long! The following weekend, our client's wife asked her husband to baby-sit while she went shopping. To ensure that she actually went shopping, our client requested she buy him a shirt from his favorite store.

Sprinting toward a men's store with us in hot pursuit, she purchased a man's shirt within minutes. Throwing the package into her trunk, she sped out of the mall parking lot. Within twenty minutes of leaving her house, she had bought a shirt and parked her car in front of a large hotel. Entering the hotel lobby, we spied her standing at the front desk opening a bright pink envelope and extracting a key.

With a smile on her face and a room key in her hand, she sauntered toward the bank of elevators. With our hidden camera rolling, we coincidentally chose the same floor. Exiting the elevator and glancing at the key in her hand, she turned down the hallway. Before the door of room 202 closed, we heard a male voice say, "It's nice to finally meet you." Her Internet affair had blossomed into an actual meeting.

Our next strategy was to call the husband. Within minutes he stormed through the hotel lobby, mumbling that he had left his children in the car out front of the hotel. We are never surprised at what any day holds, and this was no exception. That day, we added "babysitter" to our repertoire. Marnie dashed out to the car to stay with the three scared kids, while Ali guided our client to the clandestine hotel room. After much screaming and yelling, our client stumbled down the stairs toward the lobby, with his wife not far behind. Racing across the tile floor, she mumbled something about "He was just someone to talk to!" Our client just shook his head and drove away, hardly giving his new-found babysitter time to get out of the car!

> *E-Adventure*
> *George: I'm really looking forward to meeting you. Until Thursday.*
> *Lisa: I can hardly wait for our new adventure.*
> *George: I remain incredulous, but at least accepting now of the rapid e-tidal wave of emotions that have beset my life.*
> *Lisa: Until Thursday.*

Whatever the definition of adultery is, once a person invests time, and starts writing secret and exciting words to a stranger, a full-blown affair is imminent. The novelty of the chat line will fade, and the desire to meet face-to-face is the next step. Your mate could be only a "click" away from adultery. A person can forget the daily drudgeries, such as the dirty laundry, mortgage payment, or the kids' doctor's appointment. E-mail intimacy is a fantasy, not a reality.

Susan's heart raced every time she turned on her computer. She was married, but had recently started chatting online with a man. Rushing home daily to chat became a ritual. The messages were becoming more intimate, and the eventual face-to-face meeting was soon to become a reality. Susan started asking her online lover more details about himself before taking that next step. She gasped in disbelief as the realization set in that her cyber-lover was in fact her husband!

Forming a relationship or even just flirting on the Internet with someone other than your mate amounts to online adultery. Virtual infidelity can happen by just switching on your computer. Exchanging confidences with people you have never met will not relieve the tedium of a dull marriage. Make sure you put the fire out before it burns your house (and computer!) down.

> *It was love at first E-mail*
> *Angel Eyes: I can't stop thinking about you.*
> *T.J.: My wife is sleeping. I can hardly wait until she falls asleep these days.*
> *Angel Eyes: My husband is sleeping.*
> *T.J.: What are you wearing?*
> *Angel Eyes: Flannelette pajamas (LOL)*
> *T.J.: No really, what are you wearing?*
> *Angel Eyes: A tiny silk red teddy. I was at the mall today, and bought it when I thought of you.*
> *T.J.: Are we on for next week?*
> *Angel Eyes: Yes, but I just heard a noise. I better go.*

Internet affairs are a new way to commit an old sin, but really are false and as anonymous as sharing your story with someone sitting beside you on an airplane. What starts out as a titillating hobby can turn into a potentially destructive situation. The problem evolves when stressed-out people come home from a hard day, sit down at the computer, and find the energy to live out secret lives with complete strangers. If your mate has graduated from his or her digital dalliance to a real affair, be aware that obsession often wins out over judgment.

10 WARNING SIGNS OF "TERMINAL" LOVE

1. Change in sleep pattern
    Do you wake up at 3:00 am and your mate is online? Or does your mate tend to stay up later than you? The cyber love may be a few time zones away.

2. Privacy while on-line
    Does your mate do the quick-click? This is to minimize the screen when you are too close for comfort.

3. Ignoring their nest
    Are the dishes piling up, or is the lawn a foot high?

4. Multiple E-mail accounts
    Multiple identities?

5. Never wants to rent a movie
    The computer becomes the only relaxation tool they need.

6. You are jealous of the computer
    It is painful to deal with the reality that your mate prefers the company of the computer.

7. You overhear something strange as your mate quietly talks on the phone.
    "How will I know you, or what do you look like?"

8. Suddenly your mate is flying to a city on a business trip, but he rarely travels.
    Maybe he is meeting his cyber-love.

9. Unusual web sites are showing up on the computer's history
   Porn sites, dating services or lonely-hearts clubs

10. Check the credit card bills for unusual purchases.
    On-line services often cost money to subscribe.

10 REASONS NOT TO HAVE AN AFFAIR

1) Financial drain

2) Embarrassment

3) Divorce court

4) Custody consequences

5) Job loss

6) Tarnished reputation

7) Guilt

8) Sexually transmitted disease

9) Being ostracized from family

10) Loss of self-esteem

LIVING WITH INFIDELITY

Marriage has a 50% survival rate. If you were told that you had a 50% chance of survival getting onto an airplane, would you fly? The statistics are terrifying. Re-evaluate your expectations of marriage if you are to continue your relationship. Remember the beginning of your relationship? That intoxicating and exhilarating feeling of love? Your mate's adultery made all those feelings come crashing down around you. That particular period of your relationship as you knew it has died. Hard as it may seem, this is now a chance at a new beginning. The transition will be rocky and emotional. Repairing a relationship that has been shattered by infidelity is a long and painful process. Accept that things may not be right for awhile.

My life was typically normal. I had a wife, two kids and a dog. We had worked hard so my wife could stay home with the kids. I would work long hours to provide for my family. I had just recently received a promotion, and we were all looking forward to the future. All my friends tell me that I shouldn't blame myself, but I feel I contributed to my wife's infidelity. I started working longer hours and had to bring work home consistently. I feel I was not there emotionally for her.

One day at work I received a phone call from a woman whom I did not know. She was very adamant that she meet with me. I asked her to come to my office later that day. What she had to tell me knocked me over. She suspected her husband, who was a postal worker, was being unfaithful to her. She had hired investigators to tail him. The investigators found him on more than one occasion at my house, doing more than delivering mail! She presented me with a picture of my wife and her husband in an embrace at the front entrance of my home.

In a blinding daze, I went home. I took one look at my wife, and immediately she knew that I knew. The ensuing months were the hardest that I have ever had to endure. We definitely had the most turbulent time, but both of us wanted our family to make it.

Through constant counseling to rebuild

*our family, we have managed to work
things out. Both of us are not the same
people who got married 15 years ago. We
have both grown and developed into a
couple who now communicates. I always
say that I've been married twice, but to
the same woman. We feel our marriage is
stronger now, because of her affair. After
the agony we endured, we actually emerged
closer.*

Peter, married 15 years

If you have made the choice to save your relationship, WHAT
NOW? The initial shock, anger and betrayal are over, but the
incomprehensible pain still remains. The difficult task of putting
your life back together is now at hand. Where do you start?

The first person who needs looking after is you. Take charge
of your own life. Dwelling on the anger and dredging up images of
the affair are redundant. You have both decided to work on your
relationship, so throwing the affair back at your partner at every
chance will only slow the healing process. In this way, the wounds
will never heal.

Reconciliation will be slow if your emotional well-being is in
danger. The healing of an affair can be a very awakening experience, but an ordeal you can use to your advantage. The affair
happened for a reason, and therapy is strongly recommended for
both partners. A good counselor will get to the root of the problem. This is your first step in the healing process.

BE SELFISH! It is now your turn. Join that club that you
thought you could never afford. Go and buy that suit you always
wanted. What about the money your mate spent on the affair? This
is called the "ME PHASE." You will be surprised how much better
you will feel by doing a few small things just for you. If you have
always put yourself on the bottom of the scale, it is now time for

you to think about yourself and what is good for you. Your self-esteem has been destroyed. You have to build it back up little by little. It is probably the hardest road back to healing, but it is the only road.

After my husband confessed to his affair with a co-worker, we decided to try to stay together and work out our problems. However, I was completely and utterly consumed with his whereabouts for years after. If I had all the gas that I wasted driving around to confirm his activities, I could go on a trip around the world. If he said he was going to the club for a round of golf, I would drive there to confirm his story and for my own peace of mind. If he was late coming home from work, I assumed he was with her and concocted stories in my mind, which turned me into a raging lunatic. As soon as he would go to sleep at night, I would run out to his car and check for any kind of evidence of the affair still going on. I realized that as soon as he had confessed to me regarding his indiscretion, he felt at peace. I, on the other hand, had a terrible time forgiving, and even after four years, I still check for evidence every so often. My life will never be the same. I am and always will be on my guard.

Debbie, married 16 years

You will probably ask yourself over and over if you made the right decision. Remember, whenever you look at your mate or react

to something he or she says or does, the hurt will resurface immediately. To deal with your healing, you have to suppress the desire
to rehash the affair. Concentrate on the good years and the reasons
for staying together. It is painful to hear that the relationship was
not satisfying. Self-disclosure is vital to intimacy. Take all the inte-
grated parts of your marriage to create a big picture and then
FOCUS ON THE BIG PICTURE. There is a lot more there to
see than you may realize.

During this self-evaluation, you will sometimes see aspects of
your relationship which before may not have been apparent. The
bond has been broken, and you can't go back to the way things
were. You are two different people now. Until you are out of the
emotional triangle, your marriage will not move forward. Set high
standards to enhance your chances of getting what you want out
of a relationship.

*Living through an affair. What a hell
that was and still is. After seven months
of my wife's never being home, and taking
absolutely no interest in our home or me, I
knew something was wrong. I planned a
trip out of town on business, and then
hired investigators to watch my wife while
I was away. The investigators were not
bored. There was a lot of activity while I
was gone. I came home, met with the
investigators, and then invited my wife out
for dinner. I told her I knew everything.
She admitted to the affair right away, and
said that she had been really unhappy
with what she had been doing and tried to
break the affair off, but hadn't yet. She
wanted our marriage to work. There was
a wealth of emotion, and for the first year,*

> *I was extremely depressed. My wife could say little things that hurt me, and all of those images of the affair were right back in my face. When I went out of town on business, I would always have a panic attack driving to the airport, afraid she was already on the phone, making plans. It's easy to get divorced, but difficult to stay married after an affair. My wife did everything possible for me to forgive her. But after two years of my interrogating her every move, I was totally miserable, and I realized I just could not forgive her. For her sake and mine, we separated. Divorce has not been talked about, but it is a possibility. I could not get the images of her affair out of my mind, awake or sleeping. My life will never be the same. If a friend had told me that I would have to live through an affair in my marriage, I would have told him he was crazy. You don't know your own strength until you are put to the test.*
>
> *Ron, married 10 years*

Adultery destroys your faith and trust. You are now faced with the long road to slowly rebuilding it. Accepting a choice that will make your life more difficult is extremely hard. That choice probably won't be made if the bonds of love are not powerful. You have to be willing to pay the price for something that you really want. Once you have found that peace within yourself and have healed some of your pain, only then can you and your mate start rebuilding.

Looking after yourself now is most important. Do not focus on whose fault the affair was. Focus on resolving the problem and moving on. Be cheerful if it kills you, and do not mention the incident again.

An affair is often a wake-up call. Vulnerable people are easy targets. Affairs are sometimes a way to make people feel better about themselves. As one of our clients told us, when she asked her husband "Why?" he responded, "I don't know, maybe it was because she always commented on my choice of ties, and it made me feel good."

Your relationship does not have to end because of an affair. A relationship that survives infidelity can sometimes become stronger. Ann Landers wrote, "Fidelity is the glue of any lasting relationship. Without it, the relationship falls apart." She goes on to say, "Many women say their husbands stay with them because of the children." A man who engages in extramarital affairs teaches his sons that this is an OK behavior. A woman who stays with an unfaithful husband may send a message to her daughters to do the same. Children observe and sense these things at an early age. Cheating partners do not make ideal parents.

When a relationship ends, it is with a great deal of pain and with devastating consequences. Leaving a relationship after infidelity can make you afraid to enter into another relationship. It's important to first feel your pain. It's part of the healing process. You realized that your unhappy relationship wasn't going to change and that lingering sense of hopelessness set in, so you took the giant step and left. All roads to heal your heart should be explored. Put your experiences into perspective. The transition will be difficult, but not impossible. Counseling is always an option. Some of the friends you had as couples have now disappeared; maybe they took sides. You are now faced with the prospect of being alone. For a time it's wise to keep social relationships casual and seek fun and friendship. Build a new social network to see who you are now, and what you need from your next relationship.

Imagine your new life: you've been released from a negative relationship, and you're restoring your self-esteem. Negative visual-

ization can lead to negative results. Visualization can be an important tool in physical and emotional change. Visualizing yourself as
happy can motivate you to pursue happiness. You will become
much stronger when you direct your energies to making your hope
of happiness a reality.

If you've thrown yourself into a new relationship before
you've healed the wounds of a broken heart, somewhere down the
road it will haunt you. When you are involved in a rebound relationship, emotionally you are not ready to let that new person in.
You are still carrying a great deal of pain.

A WORD OF CAUTION: A new companion may not have
the magical powers to rescue you from your unhappiness, nor can
he or she take away the feelings of hurt and anger. Most rebound
relationships are transitional. The problem that usually occurs is
that people want to turn transitional relationships into permanent
relationships. This happens because people do not want to be
alone. The need to fill that emotional vacuum with new compan-
ionship and affection is powerful.

A DAY IN THE LIFE OF A P.I.

Be Prepared

BE PREPARED

Our very first case was memorable. We were hired to follow an unfaithful husband, and our adrenaline was pumping. We arrived in the district where the man lived and pulled into a 7-Eleven store to get some coffee. Since we were early, we felt we had time to relax and get organized before he left his house. Our newly purchased video camera was with us. It was a beautiful summer day, and we decided to drink our coffee outside while leaning on the car and admiring our purchase that we had set on the hood of the car.

As we were checking our equipment, out of the corners of our eyes, we saw a car that was undeniably our subject's pull out of his street and drive away. Panicked at the thought of losing him, we grabbed the camera and jumped in the car, spilling coffee over everything, and swiftly backed out of the parking lot. We put the car in drive and flew away after him, but our camera bag and one of our purses were on the hood of the car! We had to pull over and retrieve our belongings and, of course, never found our man again that day!

FLYING HIGH

A pilot's wife taught us just how important cellular bills are in solving infidelity cases. We knew within the first fifteen minutes of talking to him that his wife was the one who was flying high, not her pilot husband. Pilots are of course away a lot—that is the nature of their profession. Six months before he hired us, he had taken his wife on a Caribbean cruise, and she had told him, on the ship's deck, that she felt their marriage was dying and she needed some time alone. Of course, she told him there was no one else she was involved with. He was considering giving her the space she wanted, but there were other indicators, and he felt in his heart there was more.

After one of his flights, as he was leaving the cockpit, a flight attendant told him a joke. "When does a pilot's wife have sex? After she drops him off at the airport!" He could feel the blood draining from his face. He told us he ran to the nearest phone booth and called us.

His wife made our job easy. Her trail of infidelity was long. In the last six months, whenever our client had tried to call her on her cellular phone, it was always off. Our client told us his wife had recently taken up golfing. After studying her cell bills, it was not hard to find out where she was teeing off. The saddest part to this story was that when her husband was away flying, she would be busy organizing babysitters for their eight-year-old daughter. Adulterers can become very selfish.

On our first surveillance she led us directly to the golf course. She teed off with a man. We noticed he had on the same shirt as the rest of the staff in the pro shop, so we assumed he worked there. We waited at a table on the outside deck of the clubhouse, over-looking the 18th hole. Four long hours later, they approached the

18th green to putt out. She made a good putt and he congratulated her with a big kiss, while our video camera caught all the action.

MONEY DOESN'T BUY HAPPINESS

In the course of our investigations, we have discovered that certain age groups are more prone to affairs. A lot of women in their 30s seem ripe for affairs. A wealthy male client was totally distraught when we met with him. He thought he had everything. He had inherited a multimillion-dollar company. He had an estate home, a beautiful wife, two children and a nanny. The day he called us was the day he was served divorce papers. He had left for work at his usual time and kissed his wife and kids goodbye. He arrived at the office, and within minutes a gentleman knocked on his office door and delivered divorce papers from his wife! He had had no idea anything was wrong.

We followed his wife for seven days straight. The days our client was in town, there wasn't anything out of the ordinary. However, during his business trip out of town, a different story unfolded. The first evening we witnessed her leaving her home with a tall male. We were in hot pursuit when she went through a red light and left us in her dust. The next day we tried again. We set up the surveillance, and again we saw the two of them leave the house. With two investigators and two cars this time, she led us to the airport.

Investigators eagerly anticipate an airport arrival or departure scene. There is always an intense kiss when lovers are seeing each other again or when they are saying goodbye. They had a very long, passionate kiss in the car, but her car had tinted windows and the video was very grainy. We knew there would be another opportunity if she got out of the car, which she did. We had our camera set up behind a brick column, right in line with the car. Suddenly an airport shuttle bus drove up and blocked our view. We quickly started to run around the bus, only to see her drive off! Video is crucial in these cases, but from our description of the male, our client knew who it was. Apparently it was his brother's best friend, who certainly had less money and less class, but he obviously had something that she desired. Our client subsequently divorced his wife.

A PICTURE IS WORTH A THOUSAND WORDS

Most of our clients are extremely emotional. When do you hire an investigator? Usually when you are at the end of your rope. Some clients just want a report of their mate's activities and no video. One lady hired us to follow her boyfriend. He was with another woman. We gave our report to our client, and of course her boyfriend denied all of her accusations. We were watching him in a bar, and he told our client that she had hired incompetent investigators because they were watching the wrong guy. She was starting to believe him. This guy, however, had a very distinctive belt buckle, which we described to our client. And of course, the picture we took of him and his "friend" could not be denied.

YOUNG AND OLD

Sometimes our clients leave out pertinent information. One of our clients had a fight with his girlfriend, and unbeknownst to us, the night before the surveillance, he had told her that she had better be careful because he was going to have her followed. The next day, while we followed her from work, she kept looking in her rearview mirror. She then turned into a shopping center and made a couple of sharp turns. We suspected she was on to us and terminated the surveillance. Our client called and said that she had phoned him from her car and said that two women were following her. One was old, and the other was young! We are still trying to figure out which one of us was the old one!

HUSBAND ON BOARD

Steve overheard his wife arrange a rendezvous on the phone. The plan was to meet her lover at 12:45 p.m. at the usual place. Steve, of course, did not know where the usual place was. She did have an appointment at the physiotherapist at 12:00 noon, so that is where we set up the surveillance.

Five minutes later, to our horror, Steve pulled into the parking lot. We tried to get his attention, to no avail. To our amazement he jumped into the back of his wife's van. He then phoned us from his cell phone and told us of his plan. We told him to get out of the van and let us do our job, and that he was making a very big mistake.

Just then his wife came out of the doctor's office and jumped into her van. She drove about half a block, stopped and jumped out of the van. We held our breath as she reopened the back door slightly and then closed it again, without seeing her husband. Obviously, he had not closed the door properly. She drove to a bingo hall and again got out of her van. This time she opened the back door completely to retrieve her purse, and out fell her husband! Hardly able to drive away and trying to catch our breath in between our laughing, we left the two of them in that parking lot to work out their problems.

GOOD NEWS, BAD NEWS

A very distraught woman in her 70s came to us for help. She was in a long, loveless marriage and had started fantasizing about her high school sweetheart and former fiancé. She had recently had a facelift and looked fantastic. She told us that if this gentleman was a widower, she was going to leave her husband and contact him. Our investigation led us to the city where he lived, but we would have to find out if he was married, widowed, financially stable, etc. Initially we found that he was in fact a widower, but no other information had come in yet. Our client excitedly called us for an update. Normally we don't give out any information until the case is completed, but she was such a sweet older lady, we told her we had good news and would meet with her in two days with our findings. The good news was that he was a widower. The case progressed with information slowly coming in, only to find to our surprise that he had recently died! How were we now going to meet this lady after we had told her we had good news? We set up a meeting. She was so excited to see us and hear the good news. We sat down in a busy restaurant that was quite noisy. She immediately asked what the good news was.

We told her we had found him. Now for the bad news. I quietly said, "But I'm sorry to tell you he has recently died." She had a hearing aid and did not hear me. She was still beaming. Again, I took her hand and said louder that he had died. Still, she did not hear. I finally blurted out very loudly, "He's dead!"

We couldn't even look at each other for fear of laughing. We felt so sorry for this wonderful, sweet older lady, who only wanted a second chance in life. We certainly learned a good lesson in not jumping the gun with our information.

A FLICKERING CANDLE

"A flickering candle"? That is what Paul wanted us to look for. He was sure his girlfriend was in another relationship. He told us that when they made love, she always had candles burning in the bedroom for ambiance. This particular weekend, during our scheduled surveillance, his girlfriend picked up her male friend from the airport. He was visiting for the weekend. She had insisted to Paul that this male person was just a family friend who always stayed with her when he was in town. Paul wanted us to go to her house and watch from the alley when the lights went out to see if there were candles burning in the bedroom. With open minds, we headed out to her house and parked in the alley, which gave us a vantage point to her bedroom window. An hour after we arrived, all the lights went out in the house, except for the unmistakable glow of candles from the master bedroom! That was all Paul needed as proof.

THE CHASE IS ON

When we are on a case, anything can happen, and it usually does. This particular case originated from the United States. We received a phone call from a lawyer who wanted us to find and follow his client's husband. Apparently this man had told his wife he was going to a one-week seminar in Atlanta, Georgia. The lawyer's client was playing with her husband's e-mail and inadvertently found an e-mail with a woman's name and phone number in Calgary, Alberta, Canada. She investigated further and in her husband's car, which he had left at the airport, and for which she had keys, she found information suggesting he had headed to Calgary, not Atlanta. We quickly found where this woman lived in Calgary and proceeded to check it out.

As we were turning onto her street, we saw a car matching hers pull out of a parking spot. She had a male passenger. We immediately followed. They went for lunch, and with the photograph supplied by the lawyer, we identified him. After following them all afternoon, it was apparent she was showing him the sights of our city. We also were supplied with this woman's work phone number. After calling her place of work, we were told she had called in sick that day. They eventually went to a mall and suddenly started driving in circles. They had noticed our tail. We followed for a couple of turns, then went the other way. We decided to pick up the surveillance later, when it got dark.

The most important factor in a surveillance is that if you get noticed, leave the area immediately. Oh no, not us. We were dying for a coffee, so we stopped at a donut shop in the mall parking lot. As we were settling into a booth by a window, Marnie glanced outside to see the man and woman we were following looking in my car, and then writing down the license plate. They started to walk toward the donut shop. We had two full cups of coffee and untouched donuts. Excitedly, Marnie said, "They are coming in. What should we do?" I saw a door at the other side of the restaurant and we quickly bolted, leaving our untouched food and coffee behind, just as they were coming in.

We ended up behind a dumpster and decided to go across the parking lot to a fast-food establishment. Neither of us remembers getting across the lot. We sat at a booth, wanting our coffee we had left behind. From our vantage point, we saw them go out behind that same dumpster and then start walking toward the other businesses. My car, however, was blocked by their car. They looked for us just about every place but the one we were in. We couldn't believe they would turn the tables on us. He was the one having an illicit affair, and she had called in sick to work. They had more problems than finding out who we were.

With the car still blocked, I phoned my son to come to our rescue. He arrived and just shook his head at us. Two forty-something women, one his mother, hiding in his back seat as he drove out of the mall parking lot. We rescued the car later that night. We ended up following them for another twelve hours undetected. The next morning she drove her man to the airport, and we captured the loving departure scene on video.

The lawyer who had hired us told us that when the man arrived home to his wife and two small children, his key did not work in the door. He called his wife at work and asked her, "Why?" All she said was, "Call my lawyer, and he will tell you."

Normally, people who are sneaking around never detect someone following them, let alone turn on the investigator. We have to assume that since he was shocked at his unwelcome arrival at home, he had no idea why we were following him, but it probably didn't take him too long to figure it out after his conversation with her lawyer.

THE TIP-OFF

We always tell our clients that once they hire us, we will take it from there, and for them to stay QUIET. They don't always listen.

A prominent businessman from Chicago hired us to watch his girlfriend, who had recently moved to Calgary for a new job. He had introduced her to a few people he knew here. She evidently had started seeing one of his male friends quite frequently. We followed her from work one night, and she went directly to the house of her new friend, who was wealthy and good-looking. We reported this to our client, who was paying all her bills and living expenses. He couldn't believe it and thought that she was there just talking because she was lonely. We followed her night after night, always to the same house.

Finally, our client confronted her. She denied it, but he said that he had hired investigators to follow her. He again wanted us to keep up the nightly surveillance, but after he tipped her off to our existence, we couldn't continue. If he had kept quiet, we could have gotten him all the information and more that he needed.

SMILE FOR THE CAMERA

An Asian lady wanted us to monitor her husband. He worked in Chinatown, and we set up the surveillance for the following weekend. She supplied a picture of him, but then asked if she could come along, because she said that to us "white people," all Asian people look alike, just as all of us "white people look alike to her"! We did take her along the first night, with her cowering in the back seat. We followed him all over the city, with her telling us not to get too close. Of course we lost him. The following night, we decided to head out on our own. After tracking him to a house, we phoned our client and relayed the devastating news. Not completely satisfied, she requested a picture of her competition.

One of us went to the door on a pretext of looking for a lost dog, while the other was in the car, trying to capture on video the person who answered the door. However, this lady, who was also Asian, could not speak English and would only stay behind the door. We asked her if she had seen a lost dog, and all of a sudden, she produced a telephone for us to use. Obviously she did not understand. We were getting very frustrated, so with Marnie at the door using the telephone, I got out of the car in hopes of getting closer to obtain the crucial video. The woman saw me, was intrigued by the camera, and emerged outside, actually posing for a picture!

NAME THAT TUNE

We end up in all kinds of situations, and this one is memorable. Tracking a lady to a community hall led to an interesting evening. She went inside, as did about fifty other people. We could hear music playing and reported to our client. He wanted to know what the function was and asked if we could gain entry into the hall. We went into the lobby of the hall and then into the washroom. A woman was in there, looking for a telephone booth. I produced my cellular phone and offered it to her. She asked if we were part of the function. We said that we were waiting for some friends to join us.

We waited another half an hour, to determine our strategy, when the same woman appeared and asked if our friends had come yet. We said we had no idea where they were, and perhaps we should just leave. She became adamant that we join her group. We had no idea if this woman we had originally been following was part of this particular group or not. She asked our names, and I blurted out "Linda," with Marnie quickly saying she was "Judy." With no invitations in hand, we followed our new friend to her table. The woman whom we were following was seated at the table directly behind us.

We were introduced to our table and quickly discovered the event was being put on by a local radio show. It was a weekend ritual they called "Name That Tune." Every table was a team. When the disk jockey played a few bars of a particular song, each team had to shout out the name of the song. There was a host who walked around with a microphone and kept things lively. At one point, one of the ladies at our table was trying to get "Judy's" attention. Marnie had obviously forgotten the name she had given. The woman kept calling her name. Marnie was too far away for me to get her attention. Finally this woman said to me, "What is wrong with Judy?" I told her she had a hearing problem!

Both of us were occupied trying to keep tabs on the woman we were supposed to be watching. The host had a solution for people who were not joining in, or very vocal, as we found out. I was oblivious to the action, because I was intently watching our subject dancing, when all of a sudden the music stopped and I heard the host on the microphone yelling, "LINDA, GET OVER HERE!" I hoped that there was another Linda in the crowd. I waited for her to get up. The host appeared at my side and said that the penalty for not paying attention was to get up in front of the crowd and guess the next song, and then dance to it. ALONE!

When conducting cases, the only way to get information is by being discreet and staying in the background. Now here I was, singled out by the host. I did as he asked and slowly got out of my chair. The crowd, including the woman we were supposed to be watching, were now all chanting feverishly, "GO LINDA GO, GO LINDA GO," over and over again. I glanced at Marnie, also known as "Judy" when she remembered her name, who also was shouting "Go Linda Go," with a huge smile on her face.

MOONLIGHTING

Our cases don't always deal with domestic deceit. We offer a number of other services, which can lead to a variety of unusual circumstances. We were hired by a gentleman who owns two restaurants. One of the restaurants he owns outright, and the other one he owns with a partner. He wanted us to check out the partner in the other restaurant. He suspected that his partner was not putting all the money in the cash register, and he also was curious to know how he hired personnel.

Our job was to do a "money drop," which is where one person goes in and pays for something, but acts like they are in a hurry and does not wait for the change. The other person watches where the change goes. In the cash register, or maybe in the suspect's pocket? The one who was watching where the money went then approached the partner about getting a job. During the course of the job interview, the partner hired our investigator!

The crazy part came when we called our client to tell him our investigator had gotten the job. He wanted to know how his partner had conducted the interview and other details, and then asked the investigator to phone the partner back, saying she had accepted a job elsewhere. Our investigator had used a fake name and resume, but with an active telephone number. The phone rang and it was our client, but he was asking to speak to the person on the resume. He wanted her to come in for an interview. He didn't realize it was the investigator he was phoning. The resume was obviously very good, because our investigator had two potential job offers from both partners within 24 hours. At $5.50 an hour, how could she refuse?

A HEART IS BROKEN

Ask an affluent client of ours if money makes you happy, and the first thing he will tell you is "Absolutely not!" Money gives you the freedom to fly all over the world and buy whatever you want, but the lonely feeling follows you wherever you go.

We both remember the evening Clarence phoned and said his girlfriend had just recently left him to pursue a new career in our city. She was the woman he had been with for three years and he had thought was his life partner. He strongly believed that there was something or someone more than her career that she was after. Following her for three weeks did not reveal much. She liked to drink a lot and did not like to spend much time at home in the condo Clarence had bought for her. She also left her rented car, paid for by her boyfriend, at various bars and restaurants overnight whenever she was with a group of people. She liked to stay with friends because she drank too much to be able to drive. If people are constantly doing the party scene, their defenses weaken, and they often fall into the arms of trouble.

Another pattern was beginning to emerge. She would often go for drinks with the people she worked with. On one occasion she told Clarence that a group of ten people from work were going for drinks. We tailed her to the bar, and there was only a group of two. It was her and her married boss.

That night marked the beginning of her affair with a married man, and our client's ride on the emotional roller coaster. At the end of the evening, her boss drove her home and they both went into her condo. They were holding hands and trying to keep each other from falling down. We spent the night, and so did he. We caught this man on video coming out of the condo at 6:30 a.m. They had many clandestine meetings. We were kept on the case for two more weeks, and every time we followed her, she was with her married lover. Eventually the affair was exposed. Clarence contacted the lover's wife, and Clarence then ended his relationship with his girlfriend.

UNHAPPY NEW YEAR

There are more explosions than just firecrackers on New Year's Eve. This is typically a busy night for private investigators. People like to have fun that night, and of course they want to be happy. You would think that being married for ten years would give you the right to know what your husband is doing on New Year's Eve. When Michelle asked her husband what he was doing that night, he replied that it was none of her business. She had spent quite a few nights alone, and he would never tell her where he was going and with whom. She had also found a receipt for an expensive piece of jewelry that she had never received.

We followed him from home right to the apartment of another woman. The two of them emerged twenty minutes later. She was dressed to kill. We followed them to a fancy restaurant, where they wined and dined. We covertly videotaped the entire scene, catching the hand-holding with her diamond ring glittering, and the two of them gazing into each other's eyes. When we knew we had sufficient video evidence, we took the tape to our client. She previewed it and immediately called her two brothers and her husband's three brothers. They waited patiently at the front door for his arrival and subsequent departure.

Sparks also flew on another New Year's Eve surveillance. Debby called for our help. Her husband was in our city on business and had to work on New Year's Eve. She engaged us to see just what kind of work he was actually doing. We followed him from his hotel, and he drove directly to a house. About an hour later, he emerged with a woman. They drove to a video store with us right behind them. We overheard them talking about other movies they had previously seen together. Obviously this affair had been going on for awhile. They left the video store and purchased a bottle of champagne to ring in the New Year. Little did he know how his new year's resolutions would suddenly change after we spoke to his wife!

IS THERE A DOCTOR IN THE HOUSE?

It was late in the day. All the offices were closed, but one light was still burning in our tiny office when the phone rang. A deep voice quivered on the other end. He desperately needed our help but wouldn't give any particulars over the phone. He wanted to meet right away. We agreed and hung up the phone. Only knowing his first name and a vague description, we nervously set out for the meeting place. He was hard to miss: 6'6" tall and pacing. He quickly asked if we could drive to a small town 1½ hours away where his girlfriend lived. Before we could answer, he opened the back door of our car and jumped in. Marnie positioned her rearview mirror to keep an eye on him, while I tried to get more than one-word answers. We both were nervous about this tall stranger. He told us that two weeks ago, he had caught his girlfriend with another man. She had apologized and promised it would never happen again.

We tried to keep the conversation going. I asked what he did for a living. He replied, "I don't want to go there right now." I asked his name. He would only give his first name. We were getting frustrated and thinking that we were crazy for having this man in our car, when all of a sudden he put his hands in the air and said, "Okay, I am a doctor!" We looked at each other. I asked him where he practiced, and again he said he didn't want to go there. After ten minutes of silence he blurted out the hospital where he worked. I then tried to find out his girlfriend's name. Nothing. He decided to talk about the weather, and in conversation he let a woman's name slip. I asked if the name he had said was his girlfriend's. He was shocked and asked how we knew!

Arriving at our destination, he directed us to her home, but her car was not there. We then went downtown and located her car at a local lounge. We left him in the back seat of the car and went in, leaving the keys in the ignition as it was bitter cold. We never thought about leaving a stranger in the car with the engine running. Inside we found his girlfriend, but not with a man. We were getting hungry and thirsty. Time went by and we realized we had been in the lounge drinking and eating for over an hour, when Marnie said, "Do you realize we have a doctor sitting in the back seat of my car?" We paid our bill and packaged up the leftover pizza. The car and the doctor were still there. We gave him the leftovers and told him his girlfriend was with a female friend. He felt so much better, and he started talking, and talking and talking… all the way back to our office.

Ten minutes out of the small town, our passenger asked if we could stop so he could go to the bathroom. He got out of the car and stood on the highway, yelling back at us not to drive away and leave him stranded. We yelled back that he hadn't paid us yet, so we were not leaving him anywhere. That broke the ice, and he told us more than we ever wanted to know, including his pager number and his unlisted telephone number.

NICE GUYS FINISH LAST

Sometimes an affair is a very one-sided opportunity for a lusty lover. Eric had been dating a woman for two years but had never been invited to her home. Most recently she was always too busy to see him. Thinking back over the two years, he started to realize there were some major problems. Besides never going to her home, his outlay of money was getting out of hand. The last straw was when she called him to help her out one afternoon. She said she was tied up and needed to pick up her dog at the vet. Eric volunteered and headed to the veterinary clinic. After retrieving the dog and paying $1500 for the honor, he took the dog back to his place. His girlfriend arrived and picked up the dog, leaving him with a kiss, but not a check.

Our investigation revealed she had been married for four years and was still living with her husband. Obviously this affair she was having was about maintaining her lifestyle.

PHONE SEX

Happily married for 25 years until that fateful day at the gas station, while Jim was outside fueling up and his cell phone rang. His wife Sandy answered, and on the other end was a gentleman who claimed his wife was having an affair with Jim. He had really called to speak to Jim, but when he found out he had reached Jim's wife, he couldn't stop talking. Jim and the caller's wife had even advertised in a sex magazine for group sex. Unable to speak, and shaking uncontrollably, Sandy hung up the phone and said she would have to call him back. When she called him back he told her everything he knew. But Sandy still needed her own proof and hired us to follow Jim. We tailed him to an adult movie store.

After we gave Sandy this damning information, she started looking for other things. In his trunk were at least 100 porn movies. When she confronted him, Jim promised to end the affair and seek counseling. Even though the affair ended, Sandy is still dealing with Jim's sexual deviances and the sting of betrayal.

A DAY EARLY AND A DOLLAR SHORT

Joanne sat at our boardroom table explaining a highly crafted sting. We were intrigued. Would it work, or would she be wasting her money?

Joanne's husband was away on a business trip, due back Saturday night at 9:00 pm. Her elaborate scheme had us at the airport 24 hours early. An eerie feeling had come over her after speaking to him earlier that day. Joanne couldn't put her finger on what had made her feel that way, maybe just woman's intuition. When she called her single girlfriend to catch a movie on Friday night, Joanne's strategy suddenly became very apparent in her mind. Her friend seemed cold, distant and regrettably very busy on Friday night. We simultaneously staked out the airport and the girlfriend's house.

At 9:00 pm Friday night, in one corner of the city a garage door opened, and in the other corner of the city, a plane landed. Our voices crackled through the radios updating our positions, realizing we were all heading toward the same hotel. As the two lovers slowly closed the hotel room door, we rushed to inform Joanne of her excellent instincts. Her mission was not yet complete.

On Saturday night at 9:30 pm, another garage door opened when her husband finally arrived home from his dreadfully long business trip. Inside he encountered a pile of his belongings. Because his time of arrival was a day early, Joanne's mendacious husband will be a few dollars short!

BIG SCREEN TV

Another case, another husband. This husband played in a band, and his wife suspected he was having an affair with a groupie during the breaks. Arriving at the function, we found more than 1000 people there. At first we thought it would be impossible to keep track of him in that crowd. Armed with a picture of our man, we made our way to the stage to identify him. The client hadn't told us he was the lead singer! To the left of the stage was a 40-foot TV screen. To our disbelief, our subject, all forty feet of him, was shown on the large TV screen all evening, even during the breaks. To make our job easier, we captured a long, romantic kiss on the 40-foot screen. Got to love technology!

FUR-GIVE ME

Mary's future was clutched in her shaking hand as she dashed into our office. A crumpled receipt she had found in her husband's wallet for a $10,000 fur coat fell to the floor. Trying to catch her breath, Mary explained that her birthday, anniversary and Christmas had just recently passed. Our task was to snare which "fox" was wearing the coat.

The trap was set the following day at the scoundrel's office. The lunch crowd spilled onto the cold, blustery street, when out came the "Fox and the Hound." To our astonishment, the scoundrel's secretary was draped in fur. Hunting season for Mary's husband was now over.

PROSTITUTE RUNNER

On a sunny Saturday afternoon, following an older gentleman didn't set off too many alarms. He headed downtown and drove around in circles. While trying to decipher what he was doing and getting dizzy, his wife called. Informing her that we thought her husband might be lost, we explained the district he was in. Jackie said, "The old bugger isn't lost, he's picking up prostitutes!" Sure enough, around another corner, he stopped and picked up a tall 6' blonde with 5" heels. His excuse to his wife was that he had picked up this woman because she had broken her arm and needed a ride to her apartment. He couldn't explain the video of him coming out of the apartment thirty minutes later with his fly open.

A CASE OF TWO TIMING OR TIME AND A HALF?

Patricia had known for a long time that her marriage was in jeopardy. No communication—no sex—no time for the children and no time for her. Not able to endure another lonely day of his working overtime, she started snooping. Even though he guarded his truck with his life, she was able to make a duplicate of his truck key. One night while he slept, Patricia crept into his truck, and lying neatly on the seat was her evidence: a love letter from "KATHY"! She knew he worked with a Kathy.

Our opportunity came very quickly. He told her he would be

working overtime the following Monday and would be home at 6:00 pm. Promptly at 2:30 he left work and drove to a local bar. There he met a female. A quick call to their office revealed Kathy had left early that day because of a headache. After two hours of their making out in the bar and in her car, we followed him home. Patricia confronted her husband, and now he can work overtime anytime!

DOG DAY AFTERNOON

"Honey, I'm taking the dog for a walk." "Sure, sweetie." Sounds reasonable. Even nice of your spouse. But one night while following a wayward wife on surveillance, we found that she was the lucky dog.

Not five blocks from home, she met up with another dog walker, only it was a he. There was a brief kiss on the corner before they strolled to the local motel two blocks ahead. We couldn't believe it when they tethered both dogs to a tree and sauntered into the motel. One hour later, appearing disheveled but satisfied, they sheepishly untied their pooches and walked back to their own houses. Perfect alibi! Only gone a little over an hour to walk the dogs. In the divorce settlement, hopefully the lovers were dog meat!

THE THRILL OF THE CHASE

We have to put our personal feelings aside about that devious, scheming, gold-digging home-wrecker and conduct the job with professionalism when a mistress hires us. The mistress notices the same signs and excuses that used to be directed to his wife. Is she being replaced? Absolutely. Those stolen moments are now few and far between. The mistress has been replaced.

I was having a torrid affair with my next-door neighbor. I couldn't believe what I was doing. But I couldn't stop myself. My husband had no idea, and neither did my lover's wife. We would synchronize our watches and go for a late-night walk, ending up in the park. It was so exciting. Until a flashlight stopped us cold. The police officer shook his head and said that he couldn't believe people our age were in the bushes and to go get a room. I was mortified and decided the affair was over. I loved my husband and family, and nothing was worth risking that. My married lover is on to someone else, and his wife is none the wiser.

Jody, married 12 years

110 WAYS TO BE YOUR OWN DETECTIVE

1. Have you ever found a gift that was hidden, but not your size or style?

   He was going to surprise you at Christmas, but you found it in February!

2. Has your mate all of a sudden become very fashionable? Where are the sweat pants and jeans?

   Always has to look nice for that new love!

3. Watch for a change in diet. Eating salads, perhaps rarely eating at home.

   Mid-life crisis. Is he or she having meals with someone else?

4. Does your mate always have an excuse not to attend planned social or family events?

   If your mate is not interested in you, he or she is probably not interested in your friends.

5. RECEIPTS? Check them all.
    Were you at that restaurant with your mate?

6. Has your mate ever been out all night? What is his/her excuse? Phone to confirm the story.
    Call everyone you can think of. Somebody knows something!

7. Are you seldom invited to office functions?
    This could mean an office romance.

8. Look at your lover's back. ANY SCRATCHES???
    When was the last time you had wild, passionate sex?

9. Is there an unfamiliar fragrance on your mate's clothes?
    Is the scent either yours or your mate's?

10. Does your telephone ring and the caller hangs up?
    Does it only happen to you? If your mate just left, someone is calling to see if he or she is on the way.

11. Does your mate give too many details when asked simple questions like, "Where were you?"
Bells should be going off in your head.

12. Definite change in sex pattern.
Have you been asked for something out of the ordinary?

13. Have you ever entered the room while your mate is on the phone and the conversation ends with "ME TOO"?
What does your mate say when you say "I love you"?

14. Has your mate ever called to say "I'll be late" and it sounds as though he/she is whispering, or maybe just woke up?
Where is he or she calling from?

15. Has your partner ever refused to say "I love you" over the phone?
Maybe someone else is in the room, and he or she can't talk right then.

16. Has your mate suddenly become obsessed with his or her appearance?
Perhaps a new hairdo? Or for the men, maybe a ponytail? New clothes, etc.? WHY?

17. Is your mate critical? Never has a nice thing to say?
Maybe he or she is comparing you to someone else.

18. Has your partner become engrossed in a new hobby, one that you are not interested in?
    More time away from home!

19. Are the things you said that used to be cute and funny now irritating?
    It often happens when your mate is tiring of you.

20. Does your mate come home smelling like he/she has just showered?
    Doesn't everyone come home after a long, hard day smelling sweet?

21. Is your mate reminiscing about events that you did together, but you weren't there?
    Possibly remembering events that were with someone else.

22. Have you ever found a change of clothes in your mate's car?
    There is always evidence in the vehicle!

23. Does your partner carry a toothbrush, as well as having one at home and in the car?
    Always has to have that fresh breath!

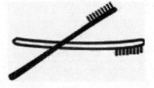

24. Is there anything unusual in your mate's address book or Day-Timer?
    Remember, it may be in some kind of code.

25. ON PAYDAY! How much has been deposited?
    Keep your eyes open... know your finances!

26. Have you noticed any unusual withdrawals from your bank account?
What is he or she buying?

27. Does the pager ring in your presence and your partner doesn't return the call?
Check for coded messages, such as 222 means meet me at 2:00 at the usual place.

28. Where are the cellular phone bills? Have they been hidden from you?
The evidence is often hidden at the office.

29. Does the passenger seat of your mate's car need adjusting when you get in?
Someone else has been riding in the car with your mate!

30. Is your partner suddenly receiving gifts and answers off-hand-edly when you ask where they are coming from?
Secret Admirer?

31. Are you being showered with surprises and presents, without an occasion? Guilt—suddenly every day is Christmas!
    Guilt comes in many forms.

32. Has your partner accused YOU of cheating?
    Trying to justify what he or she is possibly doing.

33. Have you planned a nice evening and your partner tries to start a fight?
    This could be an excuse to leave the house!

34. When you enter the room and your mate is on the phone, do you hear YES, NO, MAYBE or some other signal language?
    This is a clue that he or she can't talk since you have entered the room.

35. Is your mate in a heated discussion on the phone, and they abruptly end the conversation when you come in the room? This could signal that some demands are being made.
    When are you moving out? Why can't I see you tonight? When are you going to tell him/her about us?

36. When you leave the house does your mate ask you how long you are going to be gone and exactly where you are going?
    Maybe he or she wants to go and spend some time with their love!

37. Has your mate been married before?
    Why is he or she divorced?

38. Is your partner very quiet around you and doesn't wish to plan anything in the future?
    Perhaps you are not in the future!

39. Have you found Viagra pills?
    Who are they for?

40. Does your partner avoid your eyes and never look at you when talking?
    Maybe gazing into someone else's eyes.

41. Press re-dial on your mate's cellular phone after any unusual call.
    It won't be Pizza Hut.

42. Does your mate always have his or her cellular phone off or on vibrate?
    Checking for messages constantly?

43. Have you contracted an unexplained STD?
    What else would you need to know?

44. Is your mate distant and preoccupied with outside interests? Comments and actions that are out of character, or making casual comments about new, unfamiliar interests?
    Baseball is out, opera is in.

45. Are clothes missing?
    Whose closet are they hanging in?

46. Does your mate have an obsession about checking his or her e-mail?
    Cyber love?

47. Is your mate missing consistently on the same day or night of the week?
    Tuesday night bridge club?

48. Quick-clicking. Does your mate frantically click the mouse when you enter the room?
    Does he or she have a strong desire for more than usual privacy while online?

49. Have you found any receipts for gas or restaurants that are on the other side of the city?
    Are there no gas stations in your neighborhood?

50. Does the dog get more walks than normal?
    The dog is more confused than you are.

51. Check the mileage on your mate's car.
    One hundred miles for a gallon of milk?

52. When your mate works late, there are no incoming calls accepted at the office.
Yeah, right!

53. Does your mate wear a favorite article of clothing on certain days of the week?
Honey, where is my blue shirt?

54. Your mate doesn't give the location of meetings, who he or she are with or what time they will be home.
The Palm Pilot is missing again!

55. Has your mate asked for "space" or "time-out"?
Tell them to go stand in a corner!

56. Does your mate's mail suddenly stop coming to the house? Maybe there is a mailbox elsewhere?
Check the key ring for a mailbox key.

57. Does your mate tell you he or she doesn't want to be married anymore, but nothing is going on?
And Elvis has left the building!

58. Does your mate listen to different music now?
Country is out and opera or jazz is in?

59. Is the wedding ring suddenly in the jewelry box?
It gives me a rash!

60. Has your mate started hot waxing?
Something new.

61. Does your mate suddenly have a new outlook on life's strategies?
    Saving the children in Ethiopia?

62. Silence when you pick up the phone.
    There is more than trouble on the line!

63. Does your mate insist on answering the telephone?
    Get out of my way!

64. Check the re-dial on your mate's cell phone.
    Whom did he or she call on the drive home?

65. Is your mate's vehicle always kept free of your and the kids' belongings?
    Heaven forbid you are married, 50ish and have a family!

66. Is your mate using the bank machine more often than normal?
    Love transaction!

67. Does your mate defend others who have cheated?
    But he is such a nice guy!

68. Has your mate befriended others going through a divorce?
    Let's stick together!

69. Has your mate taken a new interest in your schedule?
    Pencil me in.

70. Does your mate encourage you to visit your friends and parents out of town?
    The first train to Clarkesville!

71. Does your mate's work schedule vary?
    Busy, busy, busy.

72. Have you received a gift from your mate that reflects a new level of tastes?
    Champagne on a beer budget?

73. Has your mate started using new words and phrases?
    Your love may be in "Jeopardy."

74. Does your mate use pre-paid calling cards for the first time ever?
    Communication is vital to an affair.

75. Has your mate started attending out-of-town seminars and conventions?
    All play and no work!

76. Does your mate come home more often smelling of alcohol?
    Eau de "Crown Royal."

77. Is your mate more possessive of his or her wallet, purse or briefcase?
    Suddenly it is under the pillow while your mate is in bed.

78. Your partner tells you he or she doesn't want a family anymore.
    We didn't know that was an option!

79. Have you ever heard someone else's name being called out during sex?
    I'm coming home, Doris!

80. Does your mate whisper while on the phone, or move into another room to talk?
    "Faster, Faster!"

81. You are losing weight and not eating.
    Because your mate is never home for supper!

82. You have noticed your mate's vehicle parked in an unusual place.
    Motel 6?

83. Has your spouse ever talked about a movie he or she had been to but you have not?
    A double life is confusing.

84. Has your mate suggested that you open up separate checking accounts?
    What's yours is ours, but what's mine is mine.

85. Does your mate now care how their breath smells? Are there new mints or gum in his or her pocket?
    Double your pleasure.

86. Have you found anything unusual in your mate's car?
    Lipstick, sunglasses, scarf, earrings, matches, etc.

87. Your mate starts sleeping so far on the other side of the bed, just about ending up on the floor.
    The deep freezer is now in the bedroom!

88. Does your partner express opinions on subjects that he or she never had an interest in?
    Protecting the rain forest!

89. Your partner is NEVER home.
    We guarantee he or she is somewhere warm!

90. Has your mate told you he or she never did love you?
    You are definitely on the back burner! Who is on the front burner?

91. Your mate doesn't want to talk about anything.
    Leave me alone, nothing is wrong!

92. Any excuse to get out alone.
    I ran out of dental floss!

93. Is there one phone number your mate is calling over and over?
    When you are having an affair, communication is vital!

94. Is your mate's cellular phone ringing more than usual?
    Does your mate usually ignore the calls when you are near?

95. You walk into a room when your mate is on the phone and you hear, "I have to call you back."
    Why is he or she whispering?

96. Are your mate's cellular bills unusually expensive?
    If your mate is not calling you ten times a day, who is he or she calling?

97. Is your mate ignoring his or her own nest?
    Are the dishes piled high? Or the lawn dreadfully neglected?

98. Have you been told your mate is cheating?
    Have you ever listened to those subtle hints you have ignored from your friends?

99. Are you the only one putting effort into the relationship?
    Always giving but never receiving?

100. Does your mate make too many promises that are never kept?
    "I promise I will stay home more," or, "Next year we will take a vacation..."

101. Do you wake up at 3:00 am and your mate is online?
    Cyber sex?

102. Has your mate tried to rationalize his or her behavior?
    I am busy at work and have too much on my mind.

103. Does your mate all of a sudden have frequent errands?
     Filling up the gas tank when it is only half empty, washing a clean car, or finding tools with price tags still on piling up in the garage?

104. Does your mate discourage you from visiting his or her workplace?
     The love triangle?

105. Do your mate's co-workers avoid you?
     From the boardroom to the bedroom?

106. Have you noticed your mate on the phone as soon as you leave the house?
     Come back in unexpectedly.

107. Has your mate been hiding his or her wallet, briefcase, or purse?
     Parking receipts have the time, date and place.

108. Has your mate suggested you go on a trip... alone?
     When the cat's away...

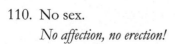

109. Has your mate suddenly joined a health club?
     Tennis anyone?

110. No sex.
     No affection, no erection!

30 REASONS TO HIRE A PRIVATE INVESTIGATOR

A private investigator:

1. can expose the affair immediately.

2. uses state-of-the-art equipment for surveillance. A picture is worth a thousand words.

3. avoids involving family and friends to follow your mate.

4. is emotionally uninvolved and remains an unbiased party.

5. will assure you of complete discretion and confidentiality.

6. is trained in vehicle pursuit.

7. will conduct the investigation with due diligence to protect the interest of the client.

8. will only release confidential information obtained to the client. This avoids gossip.

9. will provide accurate assessment of actual events, not hearsay.

10. is licensed, bonded and insured. If a court case is needed, private investigators can be called upon as reliable witnesses.

11. take evidentiary photography.

12. give you peace of mind.

13. confirm you are not crazy.

14. find out more information, such as a possible secret apartment or hangout.

15. will find out what really happens at conventions or at the bar after work.

16. will help you decide if you want to fight for your marriage or send your mate packing.

17. has access to PI firms around the world.

18. can protect the children from a custody battle.

19. can refer you to a lawyer for legal advice.

20. can ensure that when exposing the affair, the outcome will be well-planned.

21. will remove all suspicions of doubt.

22. will determine other damaging factors such as gambling, drugs or alcohol.

23. can establish the third party's background. Will your children be safe in his or her company if a divorce happens?

24. will use contacts around the world if your mate catches a plane anywhere.

25. can go virtually undetected.

26. will use their expertise and knowledge to gain access to private information.

27. will recognize and determine your mate's pattern of behavior.

28. can advise strategy and clues to assist with the investigation.

29. will conduct the case in an honorable manner.

30. will find the truth!

NAUGHTY OR NICE?

Affairs intensify during the Christmas season. Christmas is a time filled with emotions and high expectations. In an attempt to fill an adulterer's loneliness, the lover is showered with sugar and spice, and you receive the leftovers.

THE TWELVE LUSTY DAYS OF CHRISTMAS

1) Making phone calls from the garage or basement on Christmas Day.
2) Going for an extended walk alone on Christmas Day.
3) Taking the dog out four times on Christmas Day.
4. Picking a fight.
5. Last-minute Christmas shopping.
6. No gift from your mate.
7. Receiving an impersonal gift.
8. Loss of appetite.
9. Won't take part in any of the Christmas traditions.
10. Having to go into the office for a few hours on Christmas Day.
11. Tells you there isn't an office Christmas party.
12. The gift that you found a receipt for was not under the tree.

All are strong signals of a forbidden affair. Sometime between opening presents and eating turkey, the lusty lovers have to discreetly bestow their own Christmas cheer.

JUSTIFYING TEMPTATION

The following are all reasons that an adulterer will try to justify an affair.

1. Desirable

   The lover is giving your mate a reminder he or she is still desirable. "You smell good" or "I love the dress you're wearing" might be words your mate hasn't heard in a long time.

2. Accidental

   Alcohol can make a shy person turn into the life of the party. Having a few drinks when you are lonely can set the mood. A conference out of town is a breeding ground for affairs.

3. Misunderstood

His or her feelings are not being validated. Affairs can start with someone crying softly on your shoulder, telling you how his or her partner does not understand him or her. Sharing someone else's problems can be overwhelming. Dealing with people's suffering can put stress on your own relationship.

4. Sexual Addiction

It is statistically true that some people are psychologically addicted to sex. Some turn to prostitutes, pornography, chat lines or even multiple affairs. Sexual addictions can become very destructive. Momentary gratification is quite often followed by remorse.

5. Low Self-esteem

Someone you met is making you feel valuable and saying all the right words. Your confidence is built up.

6. Pompous

An arrogant, overbearing, conceited person has no qualms about having an extramarital affair.

7. Mid-life

There's more hair in your hairbrush than on your head. You haven't worn a size 6 since your wedding day. Your goals haven't been realized, and the future is not shaping up the way you'd planned. You have an overpowering need to prove to yourself that you can still attract someone.

8. Monotony of Monogamy

Emotional dissatisfaction. Too many vacations, too many clothes, too much money in the bank, too many cars, nanny to take care of the kids, and a maid to clean the house. What's left? How about an exciting, passionate, wild affair? It is more exciting to meet someone in a king-size bed downtown than to crawl into your lumpy double bed and read with a tiny book light so as not to awaken your snoring spouse.

9. Opportunity
   Out 4-5 nights a week. The opportunity can present itself on any given night. The more time spent with your mate, the less chance of exposing yourself to an affair.

10. Wrong choice

    Is it possible that the walk down the aisle was the walk of torment? Many couples realize early in their relationship that they have made a wrong choice. One party never knew his or her spouse had such a bad temper or couldn't save a dime. It is easy to cheat if the interest and desire at home is "DEAD."

11. Revenge
    Your mate has an affair—so you have one. This choice is always empty, emotionless and usually short-lived.

12. Social Butterfly
    Too much socializing is a breeding ground for sex! Is it more important to attend a social function or your child's soccer game?

13. Romantic
    Some people are just romantics and think with their hearts, not with their heads. A romantic never tires of candlelight dinners, weekend getaways, walks in the park, holding hands, and the need to be together at all times.

14. Sanctioned
    An open, no-boundaries marriage, or even different-culture-

sanctioned affairs. In many cultures, affairs are acceptable. What is customary in some cultures may not be morally acceptable in other cultures.

15. Intellectual Companion
    An intellectual companion is a shelter for an affair. Office romances usually start out this way. Having someone really listen to you and validating your knowledge is rewarding.

16. Soul Mate
    The search has ended. You have found your life partner.

17. Lonely
    Loneliness is a springboard for an affair. The need for attention can trigger many emotions.

18. Affluence
    CEO's, presidents of corporations, doctors, dentists, or executives. Leading a double life is expensive. People in these positions can better afford those getaway weekends or diamond bracelets. Money and power are the ultimate aphrodisiac.

19. Philanderer
    There are people who will cheat no matter what. That is how they live their lives, with no regard for others and no guilty conscience.

20. Freedom
    No boundaries.

21. Happy!
    Selfish!! You can't be happy all the time. Having an extramarital affair will not make you happy.

GRIEVING THE DEATH
OF A MARRIAGE

When you deny that your spouse is cheating, you are only cheating yourself. Grieving is the only way to fully recover from the pain of an affair. It is the same grief as from any loss, including death.

The 4 Steps of Grief:

1. Accept the reality of the loss. (Acceptance)
2. Work through the pain. (Reaction)
3. Adjust to the person's absence. (Decision)
4. Move on. (Recuperation)

Disbelief is the first natural instinct. We all try to come up with reasons, scenarios, and maybes. Unfortunately, the inevitable is thrown in your face. Next is anger. Anger can be very potent and freeing. Finally the guilt is gone and blame shifted to the other person. Sadness comes, loneliness, possibly thinking of forgiveness or acceptance of all the blame. Eventually the outcome needed to heal completely is acceptance, and then moving on. You have to fully understand what happened that led to the end of your relationship.

Once you decide to leave your relationship, you can then begin to focus on yourself and discover life separate from your spouse. The most important step in this process is recovering your shattered self-esteem. To survive the experience, a network of friends and family is essential. Laughter and even tears are very normal and can help you heal. Friends sharing your burden can become overwhelmed, however. Be careful not to abuse your friends' kindness during this time of discovery.

Your past problems could possibly turn into an opportunity. Your recuperation can lead you to avenues you never dreamed of. There is nothing quite like personal experience to change your attitude. You are the solution to your problem.

People used to ignore or even accept what was going on behind their backs. As women have become more financially powerful, they now have a choice to leave, and many victimized men are fantastic single fathers.

Probably what we have heard too many times to count is the cheating person telling his or her mate, "I never really loved you anyway." This is a way to possibly justify the affair. There is no tried-and-true method to affair-proof your marriage. Daily neglect over the years can happen very subtly.

WE CAN'T SEE
THROUGH WALLS

Infidelity, betrayal, adultery, lust, affairs, shame, cheating, dishonesty, time-out, contrition, or mid-life crisis. No matter what the term, what garners more attention, more media coverage, and more interest than the topic of sex? Illicit sex can place most people dangerously close to the edge of no return. Most people would discover, if they were willing to face the truth, that affairs are fantasies. Marriage is a reality, but always at the mercy of intrusion. Marriage can be a daily ritual of removing temptation.

Deception and lies of everyday people, the fine line between right and wrong, and the reasons why many stray at some point in their lives are the basis of our company's success. Anyone can have a mid-life crisis, but not everyone has to have a mid-life affair. People tend to sacrifice their reputations to satisfy their own needs. The most important weapon to guard against infidelity is your brain.

What people don't face, they repeat.

The temptation of infidelity will never go away. Affair-proofing your relationship can be overwhelming. People today are looking more for personal pleasure. Being selfish. Falling in love is easy. Staying in love is hard. There is never a way to justify promiscuity. The temporary excitement of extracurricular romance with candlelight and wine is not worth the pain.

As private investigators we have gained insight into recognizing the signs of a cheating mate and have suggestions on how to deal with the relationship after the affair is discovered. Many of our clients become ambivalent because they are in relationships that have soured, and they turn to us for help. All we can tell our clients is what we see on the outside. An outward show of affection in public tells a lot. We are not psychic. We can't predict how a relationship will turn out, but we certainly can get a feel about where people are at that particular point in their lives, and if the relationship is worth saving. We can't see through walls, nor can we tell what our subjects are thinking. When we are on a surveillance, we are always trying to surmise what is going on inside, while the client is on the phone constantly conjuring up possible scenarios. When a client hires us to follow his wife for one night, and she is in a bar for four hours in a dark corner with a man, all we do is report what we see.

If only people would calculate the consequences of their actions, maybe there wouldn't be so many cheating lovers. Sometimes feelings of love and desire wane in a relationship, but trust should always be a constant. What is a more devastating betrayal of trust than infidelity? It tears at the heart and for awhile destroys your life. Most people don't go out looking for an affair, but events in people's lives can change their behavior and attitudes. Possible instigators could be too many drinks at an office party, working closely with someone of the opposite sex, a convention out of town, or a long absence from one's partner. Having a job where there is a social atmosphere (entertaining clients) and flexible hours can be an inducement for affairs.

Many of our clients freely admit that it was very difficult to make the call to hire a private investigator. Most people immediately feel guilty when they make that first dreaded phone call to us. Our main concern is always to put them at ease. Our client's main concerns are that his or her partner is going to know about us, or that we are going to give the client the evidence that has been suspected for a long time. A client's coming to us before confronting his or her mate will almost certainly guarantee that we will find something, good or bad. If we find that absolutely nothing is out of the ordinary, or that an affair is happening, either way, our clients then can make informed decisions as to what route to take.

Having friends and family doing your detective work first almost certainly leads to a dead end. It makes our job much more difficult. If a person is not trained in surveillance, it is very easy for him or her to make some big mistakes. If people who are involved in affairs even remotely suspect that they are being followed, they might cool it for awhile or be extra careful in their moves. Constantly accusing someone when you don't have all the evidence will also destroy your chances of ever finding the truth. Clients can make our job easier by helping to put the pieces together. The most important aspect of all is to KEEP QUIET. If your partner thinks that you are oblivious to his or her activities, he or she will carry on as if things are normal. Be the best actor you can be, but watch for every sign of cheating. Document everything. For instance, if your partner is late coming home from work every Wednesday, that night might be a good night to target for surveillance.

Our work has taken us to places we never thought we would be. No two days are the same. We've hidden in churches, behind trees and garbage cans, and in underground parking lots. We have attended private parties totally undetected. We have spent countless hours at the airport observing the departure and arrival scene. We have crawled out of bars on our hands and knees and even gone behind the bar to temporarily act as bartenders, quickly explaining to the real bartender what we were doing there. There have been many situations where we've had to be creative. Imagine crashing an aerobics convention smorgasbord! We stood in line with everyone, but of course there was no place for us to sit. We observed our subject with someone else while we were in line, then went into the basement of the hotel and ate our dinners without utensils.

When Backtrack Investigations Inc. first opened its doors, we had no idea of the challenges we were about to face. From our first memorable case, we have never looked back. The most satisfying aspect of our work is being able to connect with our clients in their time of need. Every time we close a case, regardless of the outcome, we have only been in the client's life a short but memorable time.

Our clients come to us as strangers, but leave as friends. Being an investigator brings out many roles. On a daily basis, we are dealing with people's emotions and the most distressing secrets in the most horrendous period of their lives. After we have discovered an affair, we offer our clients our discretion, a smile, many times a hug, and most of all, respect.

It is documented that 50% of all marriages end in divorce; 70% of those involve an extramarital affair. Infidelity may be statistically common, but psychologically unhealthy.

During our many domestic investigations, we have found that many of our clients' stories have similarities. In order to determine if our clients actually need a private investigator, we ask certain pointed questions about their mates. Our list of questions has grown over the years, but if there is an affair happening, the client's partner usually meets the profile we have outlined. Our list is a guideline compiled from actual case files. Many of these signs may apply to your partner but may not necessarily mean anything conclusive. However, they are certainly worth discussing. It is possible to carry on an affair without any tangible evidence.

As our company continues to grow, we look forward to the next phone call, when a new client gives us a heartfelt description of his or her life. We hang up the phone, grab the camera equipment, and head out the door. During our years in this profession, our clients and their varied cases have enlightened us about human behavior almost beyond belief.

The path of happiness and love would be much easier if it wasn't littered with irresistible distractions. Very few individuals recognize and accept their inability and unwillingness to maintain a monogamous relationship. Most individuals just jump off the cliff. There is an alternative. Do not let your heart control your brain. We encourage you to make a conscious decision. Eventually you will see that an affair is the worst decision to make. Never let yourself be forced or coerced into doing something that you will feel guilty for later, or have residual negative feelings about.

We are all responsible for how our relationships continue, and we have to refine and clarify our own values. Remember that there are very few relationships that satisfy all the needs of both partners. A person's unique emotional makeup may cause him or her to look for the same kind of individual he or she had in a previous relationship.

INFIDELITY. It knows no boundaries. It can happen to any couple, together for any length of time. Couples who appear to have a solid foundation can easily be affected by duplicity. When an affair is exposed, it can feel like part of your life has left your body.

In the final analysis, we have no qualms about saying that we still believe in old-fashioned romantic love. Our clients have all contributed in their own ways toward our understanding of the mystery of love.

Love is the most quintessential human emotion, and the ultimate friendship.

THE 10 STUPIDEST THINGS
OUR CLIENTS HAVE
ASKED US TO DO

1. Find the condo my husband bought for his mistress.

2. Go to my spouse's office and find his or her lover. You will know what he or she looks like.

3. I don't have a picture of my spouse, but he/she is very good looking and has brown hair.

4. I'll give you my garage door opener, and then you can open the garage door to see if my spouse has left yet.

5. I want you to videotape my own affair.

6. Rent an office in the same building as my spouse.

7. Peek into the bedroom window.

8. Call the realtor and get into the house, or call the realtor and buy the house.

9. Go to the front door and tell me if my wife has on a red negligee. If she does, she probably has a man inside.

10. Go to the airport and see if my spouse traveled with someone. I don't know what flight he or she is on.

TOP 10 OUTRAGEOUS EXCUSES

1. A husband comes home and tells his wife of ten years that he doesn't want a family anymore. Her reply is, "I didn't know that it was an option."

2. I need to be alone for awhile to find myself.

3. I just want to be happy.

4. You didn't have to ruin everyone's life when you told my lover's husband about our affair. You only had to ruin mine!

5. I am getting too emotionally attached to my lover, so I am breaking it off.

6. I was only testing you to find out if you trusted me.

7. I always remove the luggage tags at the airport before I come home.

8. A man explains that he lives with his crazy sister and that is why his girlfriend cannot come to his house. One day the girlfriend calls his house and a woman answers. She asks if this is her boyfriend's sister. The female says, "No, I am his wife!" After being confronted he says, "I told you my sister was crazy!"

9. Sit tight. I'll let you know if I am coming back to you.

10. I need time out.